TREASURES

MYRON HUMBLE

Gotham Books

30 N Gould St.
Ste. 20820, Sheridan, WY 82801
https://gothambooksinc.com/

Phone: 1 (307) 464-7800

© 2024 *Myron Humble*. All rights reserved.

No part of this book may be reproduced, stored in a retrieval system, or transmitted by any means without the written permission of the author.

Published by Gotham Books (November 23, 2024)

ISBN: 979-8-3306-0351-0 (H)
ISBN: 979-8-3306-0349-7 (P)
ISBN: 979-8-3306-0350-3 (E)

Because of the dynamic nature of the Internet, any web addresses or links contained in this book may have changed since publication and may no longer be valid.

The views expressed in this work are solely those of the author and do not necessarily reflect the views of the publisher, and the publisher hereby disclaims any responsibility for them.

DISCLAIMER

This story is fictional a product of the author's imagination. Characters are fictional and any resemblance to persons, places, and events is coincidental.

TABLE OF CONTENTS

Prologue i
Chapter 1 1
Chapter 2 7
Chapter 3 15
Chapter 4 24
Chapter 5 32
Chapter 6 41
Chapter 7 47
Chapter 8 55
Chapter 9 67
Chapter 10 79
Chapter 11 86
Chapter 12 97
Chapter 13 104
Chapter 14 123
Chapter 15 134
Chapter 16 140
Chapter 17 146
Chapter 18 157
Chapter 19 162
Chapter 20 177
Chapter 21 182
Chapter 22 192
Chapter 23 204
Chapter 24 212
Chapter 25 220
Chapter 26 232
Chapter 27 239
Chapter 28 246
Chapter 29 257
Chapter 30 263

PROLOGUE

I was wandering along the bank of the Susquehanna River near Goldsboro thinking, or dreaming, of the old days when I grew up here in Valleyview Township. Ha! Dreaming… again… that was my thing then, sixty seventy years ago. I was always dreaming. Dreaming of the future. Now, my dreams were of the past, long gone.

This is where my life began… my adventure. I was born near here in Harrisburg in 1942, but my story began… really began in 1958. The battle for my soul.

This was a farming community but most of the people around here… or many, were veterans of World War two or Korea. Dad was a WW2 vet and a leading member of the local American Legion Post. Most of the people were employed at three military bases near here, Olmstead Air Force Base across the river and New Cumberland army depot near the Harrisburg Airport… the *old* airport and the naval depot at Mechanicsburg. Olmstead had become the Harrisburg International Airport long since.

Mom, a skilled seamstress, worked at the airbase repairing parachutes, a skill she employed during the war. Dad was an aircraft mechanic, a profession he learned in the Navy.

Of course, like most if not all boys, I was mesmerized by the airplanes that flew overhead going in and out of the air base… P-51 Mustangs, my favorite, or the F-86 Sabre's. And *that* was where my mind was all the time… airplanes… or boats and ships.

I was obsessed with flying, daydreaming my life away in class, to the frustration of teachers, and the amusement of my fellow classmates. That or boats… ships. To my teachers' frustration, or amusement I was always drawing pictures of planes or ships on the edges of my papers.

My mother, however, was focused on spiritual things. Mom's frustration, and disappointment, was that I was not interested in the church or religion, and she got no help from Dad. Jesus was her heart and soul and she constantly tried to get Dad and I involved in the church.

I was interested in boats, and during the fall of 57 I started to build a boat in Dad's garage, to his annoyance. Mom used her skill to make a sail for the boat… but I digress.

My troubles began the following year, the summer of my sophomore year. However perhaps the seed was planted earlier, in grade school. I met John McCaskey who started to bully me and when I complained to the teachers, or the principal, I was told to stop whining and be a man. Dad told me to stand up for myself. So, I did… I loaded a book bag with rocks and the next time John came after me I beat him with that.

But he caught up with me, when I didn't have the bag, and in the ensuing brawl, we were both bloodied… bruises, bloody noses, loose teeth, black eyes. I am not sure who won that but since he ran off crying, I guess I can claim the win.

When John and some of his goons tried to steal lunch money from younger kids at middle school, I stood up to him and with the help of other boys, and girls, sent them running. And that was how I met Connie.

Connie, a cute girl with long black hair, tried to help, but she got into trouble. She was a fighter, but she bit off more than she could chew when she took on a big thug and I rescued her. That was my introduction to Connie McCormick. Her father was a naval officer at the naval depot in Mechanicsburg.

Later, big brother Andy, little brother Charlie, Cousin Doug from Middletown across the river, and I, ran into John's big brother, Mac and his wannabe gang of youthful thugs on River Road. Mac was older but not necessarily bigger, or wiser… or smarter. With the help of some big sticks and well thrown rocks, by Charlie, an up-and- coming pitcher in Pony League baseball, we sent them running away bloodied and bruised… and at least one broken bone.

The McCaskeys never forgot the beating they got that day, and they made trouble for us… especially me, throughout high school. I became the target of their wrath after Andy left for the naval academy.

My head was full of dreams… of airplanes, flying, and adventure. By the time I started my junior year I was well known for my ambition to fly… and to join the navy. Everything was affected by that, in my mind as well as with other students. I was too short, too weak, too dumb, not into sports… all of the usual stuff that appealed to teenaged boys. I was a loner, not involved in class pursuits… until the last two years. Then everything changed.

When I was not dreaming of airplanes, I was dreaming of Connie. Unfortunately, I was too introverted and so socially inept… no, really…

I was. After my heroic rescue of the girl nothing happened… with her or any other girl until the summer of 58. And that is where my story really begins with a dream and our sophomore class trip to Gifford Park.

CHAPTER 1

I leaned out of the cockpit of the Stearman biplane and called, "Clear!" The attendant acknowledged. "Clear!" I pressed the ignition and the radial engine roared to life. It coughed and sputtered, threatening to quit, and I adjusted the throttle and mixture until it ran smoothly. I taxied to the end of the runway and opened the throttle. The roar of the engine echoed off the surrounding woods and made my heart pound. I released the brakes and the airplane roared down the runway; the woods at the end of the runway rushing at me as the airspeed increased. I pulled back on the control stick and the biplane leaped from the grass field. I was pressed into the canvas seat as the ground fell away. I felt free.

I performed aerobatics; twisting, diving and performing loops and rolls. I swooped and climbed and saw spectators on the ground watching me in awe.

I pulled the nose up. The speed dropped as I tried to keep the plane level. It stalled and fell into a spin. My pulse pounded as I pushed the stick forward and pressed the rudder pedal. The spin stopped, and I pulled back gently on the stick, bringing the nose level. The effect of the g-forces pressing on me as the aircraft spun excited me. Eager to experience the thrill again, I climbed toward the sky.

I pulled the stick back and the nose came up. The plane slowed, stalled, and fell into a spin. I felt the rush as the airplane spun downward. I let it continue before pushing the stick and pressing the rudder bar. There was no response. The plane continued to plunge earthward. With the ground rushing toward me I was overcome with fear and panic. I frantically pushed and pulled on the controls. The thrill was gone. I was sweating and shaking as the ground hurtled toward me. My stomach churned; my heart felt like it was going to burst…

"Michael. Michael. Wake up! Your class will be here for you soon. You have to eat some breakfast." My mother, Anne Hunter, shook me awake. Mom was a five-foot-two dynamo with long auburn hair, streaked with grey, tied back in a bun. I sat up. I was sweating. "Get up!" She poked me. "And take a shower; you are covered with sweat. I don't know why. You hardly wear any covers, and this room is freezing."

I needed that shower. I got my breath back as the cold water coursed over me reviving me before it finally warmed up.

Dressed, I rushed into our large country kitchen to hear the usual refrain. "Michael, tie your sneakers before you trip and break your neck."

My father, James Hunter, was sitting in his usual spot at the head of the table, reading the morning paper. He was forty-three of medium height and he had short black hair with not a hint of grey. He was fit but showed a slight bulge which my mother ascribed to his fondness for beer.

"Good morning, Dad." I flopped into a chair. "Thanks Mom."

She gave me a puzzled look as I grinned. She set the milk on the table. "For what? Getting you out of bed? I do that every morning… or warning about your shoes? I do that *all* the time." She looked at me over granny glasses. "It's about time I got some thanks around here." Mom cast a side glance at Dad. I saw him smile behind the paper. "So, what is so special about this morning?" She asked.

"You saved my life."

"What's a mother for." She frowned, "I do *that* all the time. So, what is so special about this morning?"

"You woke me up," I grinned, "just as I was about to crash."

She shook her head, rolled her eyes, and dismissed me with a wave. "Eat your breakfast; the bus will be here soon."

Dad lowered a corner of the paper. "You need to stop dreaming and get into the schoolbooks. You need better grades if you want to be a pilot. You should follow your brother's example. He's really applying himself."

I made a face. "Can't I dream even when I sleep?" I grimaced. "Anyway, I can't be a pilot. I'm too small, and my eyesight is not good enough; I need twenty-twenty vision." I touched my glasses for emphasis and quietly mumbled. "And I'm not Andy."

"I know you're not Andy." Abruptly, he put the paper down. "That kind of attitude will not get you anywhere.

You need to get interested in those schoolbooks, especially algebra." He tapped his finger on the tabletop. "You have to go to summer school because you failed algebra this year."

"Algebra. What good is it anyway and what is it used for? A plus B equals C?"

"If it wasn't important they would not be teaching it, and you need it to graduate. You do want to graduate, don't you?" Dad said.

"Speaking of useless, I don't know what you find so interesting in those old service manuals. Those old airplanes aren't flying anymore and there are other ways to be involved with airplanes besides being a pilot. Your old man learned aircraft mechanics. I did my share of flying for three years in the Pacific. If you don't get rid of that loser attitude you will never amount to anything."

"James! That's not nice." Mom protested. "He's only fifteen. He has plenty of time. Not everyone can be like Andrew."

"Anne, he does *not* have plenty of time. He needs to think about his future and get ready for it now. He will be graduating in two years. Do I need to remind you that he has to attend summer school because he failed algebra this year?"

Mom paused but answered, "You need not remind me of that, James but it is summer, and he should have fun. He'll do better this year; won't you dear?"

I laughed and shrugged. "I guess, but do I have to worry about books and studying right now?"

"You should think about getting involved with the young people at the church, Michael." Mom said. "Many kids are helping with Vacation Bible School in July."

"The church." Dad muttered. He picked up the paper again. "I don't see what good the church will do him. They're all a bunch of hypocrites. They go to church and listen to sermons condemning drinking, gambling, and smoking and then they come to the legion and drink, gamble and smoke. Hell, they don't even wait; they are always standing around in front of the church on Sunday morning smoking like the

Steelton foundries. The churches sermonize, but when they need money, the service clubs are the first ones they hit up to demand their share of the gambling and drinking profits. Michael doesn't need that stuff."

"Worshiping God, praying, and studying the bible are important, James. Spiritual things are as important as material things. The bible says, 'layup treasures in heaven, where neither moth nor rust doth corrupt, and where thieves do not break through nor steal'."

"Hypocrites, Anne. They are all hypocrites. Michael… or Charlie… doesn't need their influence."

"I am talking about worshipping God, James, not the church. Do you think Jesus is a hypocrite? The teachings of the bible are true and good for living. Just because some men do not obey them, does not make them wrong. Jesus says we should seek 'first the Kingdom of God and all these things will be added'. You need to build on a sure foundation, Michael. Jesus is the foundation and a mind set on God is calm and able to do many things in life."

"Well, I get more done in the legion than those guys do in the church." Dad said.

"Yes, I know. All of you are proud of what you do. Pride goes before a fall, that's what Jesus said. People need to put God first, and then everything else will go better. That goes for you, as well as the church leaders and Michael and his studies… or his dreams."

"I get along fine without it." Dad said, still staring at his paper.

I did not say anything. It was all confusing to me and I often felt trapped between them. They had this discussion often, but it never solved anything. I finished my breakfast in silence.

Mom was involved with the church and bible study, but Dad wanted nothing to do with it. There was a pull at my heart when Mom talked about Jesus, but when Dad talked, the feeling melted away. I went to church with Mom, and I saw the men standing around smoking before and after church. Then they all went to the service clubs; the Legion, the Elks, or the VFW, where they drank and gambled.

Mom pressed on. "Faith played an important part in our country's history, and I would think you would be more supportive. You are involved in that memorial to the four ministers who died in the war."

Dad said. "Yes, and they were not even of the same faith: Catholic, Protestant, and Jewish."

"Our faiths are not that different, James. The Proverbs say 'trust in the Lord with all your heart and do not lean on your own understanding. In all your ways acknowledge him, and he shall direct your paths'. The Proverbs are in all our scriptures." Dad was silent. A horn sounded out front.

"The bus is here Michael; get your things." Mom said.

I got my bag and as I went out the door, Dad slipped me a ten, and smiled. "Have a good time and don't get into trouble."

"Me? Get into trouble?" I grinned looking at the ten. "I can get into all kinds of trouble with this." I hurried out the door as he smacked my backside with the paper.

CHAPTER 2

Robert Lockhart, a junior high coach, was one of our chaperones and he had the students play baseball for an hour after our picnic lunch. They planned to go swimming in Gifford Lake later.

I did not play sports, but Mister Lockhart insisted that everyone play. As usual I was the last boy picked for a team. I was persuaded to play right field. I hoped vainly that no one hit the ball at me. I *did* catch an occasional fly ball or stop a ground ball without getting hit in the face. However, I heard the disapproval of my classmates when some of them escaped my attempts to catch them. It was mostly fun, but I did not always take it that way. John McCaskey was in my class and his mockery was relentless.

I came up to bat and got a hit and made it to first base. The next batter hit a fly ball and I ran at the crack of the bat, enthusiastically rounding the bases to what I thought were the cheers of my classmates. But the cheers turned out to be jeers as I realized my mistake. The fly ball had been caught and relayed to first base. I was the third out and we got no runs, thanks to me. I felt stupid and discouraged.

Amid much well-deserved heckling from my classmates, I sulked on the bench, discouraged. Mister Lockhart came and sat with me. "Don't let the kids get to you, Michael. Everyone makes mistakes."

"Yeah, but I keep making the same mistakes. I'm just lousy at sports. I can't do anything right." I kept staring at the ground watching a bug.

"Michael, don't worry about it." He laughed. "It's just a game. Just be patient and don't be too eager."

"Yeah, thanks." I felt a little better, but I could not lose the stupid feeling, especially in front of Connie.

"I want you to switch with Peter and catch for a couple of innings?"

"*Me,* catch? You're kidding." If anything was worse than playing in the field, it was catcher.

"Yes. *You.* Don't worry. You'll be all right."

"I guess, but I'm not good at *catching*, you might have noticed." I watched the catcher on the field catch a ball and toss it back to the pitcher.

Lockhart laughed again, "You won't have to catch fly balls, just slow pitches. Besides, you didn't do that badly out there. All you have to do is keep the ball in front of you. Block it with your body. Use the chest protector."

"Ok. I'll give it a try."

"You'll be all right." He patted me on the back. He was good at encouraging kids, one of the reasons he was popular among students.

"Yeah," I muttered under my breath. "As long as I don't have to get someone out at home."

John McCaskey was on second base itching to score. A line drive was hit to deep right and John tagged up and raced around third as the relay reached the second baseman. I moved up the baseline, concentrating on the incoming ball. I heard the screaming crowd, and I heard John coming down the baseline shouting. "Get out of my way pipsqueak!"

John was a large fellow, a hard-hitting tackle on the football team and there I stood, in front of this… raging bull.

The ball hit the dirt in front of me and I blocked it, trapping it against the chest protector. John crashed into me, flew over me, and landed behind home plate. I was lying on top of the plate. I felt a lump underneath me and pulled the ball out, rolled over, and sat up on top of the plate. John reached over me, trying to touch the plate. I touched John's arm with the ball.

"Yur *out*!" Lockhart bellowed and I laughed. I wondered why I was laughing. My head was spinning, and I was in a fog. I saw fuzzy figures moving around in front of me.

"This is not good." I shook my head, which made my head spin all the more, so I sat still listening.

John was screaming. "He dropped the ball, Mister Lockhart!"

"You missed the plate, and he tagged you, McCaskey. You're out. Stop arguing and sit down."

John continued to whine. "But he dropped the ball."

Lockhart growled. "He has the ball and he tagged you *before* you touched the plate." I raised the ball over my head to show it. The sudden move sent my head into a tailspin.

John stormed off the field to a chorus of boos. I started to lie back on the ground, laughing. Mister Lockhart was not laughing as he pulled me upright. "Michael, sit up and take a breath. How do you feel?"

"I see two McCaskeys, so I must be in hell." I muttered.

He laughed and helped me stand up. He made me rest in the shade of a tree out of the sun. "You're finished for now. Have a rest, the game is about over. Keep this wet towel on your head and do not lie down. I'll send someone to sit with you."

"I don't think I am going swimming." I was steadier but my sight was blurred, and any sudden movement sent my head into a spin.

"No, I don't think so. Not right away. I'll have someone stay with you. And don't lie down." Lockhart went back to the field.

I was holding the towel to my head, covering my eyes against the bright sunlight.

"How are you feeling Michael?" My heart skipped at the sound of Connie's familiar voice. It beat a little faster when she touched my brow and adjusted the towel. "Don't lie down. You have to sit up."

"Oh… yeah. I'm Ok."

"I don't know about that. You have to be out of your mind, standing in front of that big oaf like that."

"Standing in front of a stampeding bull? Dumb does come to mind." I laughed. "So did Lockhart draft you to play nurse?"

"*Noo*. I volunteered. The game is almost over. I saw the most exciting part anyway." I tried to get up, but she touched my shoulder. "Hey, relax. You need to rest. You could have a concussion if you're seeing double."

"Seeing two of you is a bonus." I felt sheepish and silly, my face warmed and I almost swooned. I always managed to say dumb things to girls. I did not have many… or any dates.

She made a face as if in shock and covered her grin and called out, but not so loud as to be heard. "Oh my, quick, someone call a doctor. There is something wrong with Michael. He's out of his mind." She poked me. "When did you become so bold mister?" She grinned. "My brother thinks one of me is too much."

I started to say something and hesitated.

"What?"

"Uh, nothing."

"Don't give me *nothing*. I know that look. You were going to say something."

"I don't want to flatter you."

"A girl likes to be flattered… occasionally." She blushed.

"I think you're pretty… and… and I like you and I wish I weren't so… shy." I thought maybe that hit had done more damage than was apparent. I was out of my mind being so bold, certainly out of character.

Connie was about the same height as me, five foot six. She had a smooth olive complexion and hazel eyes.

Long black hair framed her face with long bangs with natural curls over her shoulders.

"Oh, thank you. I like you, too. You're not being so shy now."

"I guess not." I stared at her pretty eyes for a moment. She was sitting close as she adjusted the cloth on my head. Her fragrance, the warmth from the nearness of her body, her lovely face so close, set my heart to racing. Temptation filled my mind and I looked away, the heat rising in my face. I murmured. "It must be the sun."

She laughed. "What's wrong?"

"Nothing."

"Hey, what were you thinking?" She pretended to be insulted. "Or maybe I shouldn't ask if it was *that* terrible."

"Oh no. Not terrible… I… I don't think. I was just thinking you smell really nice and… and it would be nice to kiss you." The blood rushed to my head and a momentary haze passed in front of my eyes. I felt hot and I tried to avoid her look. "I… I sh-shouldn't have…"

She giggled. "I think I might like that."

I looked into her eyes wondering if she was serious. I glanced at the game. My face was hot as my desire took hold of me. I moved closer as she looked at the game. When she turned back, I kissed her on the lips. Before I could stop, she placed her hands on both sides of my face and held the kiss for a moment longer. My heart went wild, and I thought I was going to faint. When she let go, I was breathing heavily, and I was dizzy. I felt like I had been run over again.

I sat back trying to get my breath. I had never felt anything like that before. It was an indescribable feeling.

She had her eyes closed and she was smiling. I was going to kiss her again when she began to play with the ring on the string around her neck. She looked around nervously.

The ring meant that she was *with* someone. I said, "I shouldn't have done that."

"It's ok. It was nice. I… I shouldn't have encouraged it." She shrugged and looked away for a moment.

"You're a surprise Michael Hunter." She touched my cheek gently. "A nice surprise."

Girls came from the ball field. "Connie, are you going swimming?" She hesitated, looking at me. "Or are you busy?" Connie turned pink and they all giggled.

I felt warm but I said. "Go ahead, I'll be ok… I think." I thought I better sit there a little longer to recover from the kiss… not that I wanted to be *over* it.

She kissed me on the cheek. Jumped up and hurried away with the girls, laughing, giggling, and chattering like magpies. "Girls!" I shook my head. My head spun and I wasn't sure if that was because of the hit or the kiss. I smiled at the thought of seeing Connie in a swimsuit; she definitely looked great in a cheerleader's outfit.

She looked back, saw me looking at her, and smiled. "Don't lie down." For a moment I thought she could read my thoughts and I felt warm… and it was not the sun.

"I won't."

I was still sitting in the shade, savoring the moment when John stomped up from the field. "Uh-oh!" I thought. I looked around for a way to escape.

"Michael. Are you gonna live?" There was a note of sarcasm.

I resisted the temptation to give a nasty reply. "I'm fine. Thanks for asking." I did not think John was being sincere. John was never concerned for anyone but himself.

"If Terry catches you mess'n with his girl you won`t be fine."

I looked at him blankly and did not answer.

After a long pause John growled, "Hey dimwit, are you listening? I said…"

"I heard you. I'm sure you're really concerned for my health."

"Maybe I should do Terry a favor and clean your clock right now."

"Take your best shot." I stood up. The movement sent my head into a spin for a second, but I tried not to let it show. I was standing on a rise, and I still did not come up to John's chin.

John stood with his fist balled and his mouth open. He appeared confused. He spoke roughly. "Next time you'll get out of my way."

I did not answer.

"You dropped the ball. I know you did."

"I tagged you before you touched the plate. You do know that you have to touch home plate, don't you? I thought you knew everything."

John took a step toward me.

"*McCaskey!* What are you doing here?" Lockhart's yell froze John. Lockhart came up to us, glaring at John. "You should be on your way to the lake."

"Yeah, sure, Coach." He glared at me and growled, "I'm going to get you," as he brushed past and stomped off.

Lockhart watched John and then asked me. "How are you?"

"OK, but I don't feel like swimming. Can I hang around the park instead?"

"Yes, that would be ok. Just be back here by four."

I assured Mister Lockhart that I would be fine. I shrugged when he asked what was going on between me and John. He shook his head and went after the other kids. I stood shaking and sat down again and waited for my stomach to settle down.

CHAPTER 3

I headed for the park, intending to go to the arcade. The thought of going to the lake to see Connie and the other girls in bathing suits tempted me but the thought of running into John changed my mind. I headed for the arcade. I still had five dollars burning a hole in my pocket. As I passed the bulletin board in the central plaza, a bright yellow notice caught my eye.

LEARN TO FLY

Gifford Airpark

Fly a Piper Cub Introduction flights

$5.00 for a half hour

(Children under 14 must be accompanied by an adult)

That was way too tempting. I had five dollars, and I was fifteen; I headed for the airpark.

I stood in line waiting my turn. A security guard approached me. "What do you think you are doing here, boy?"

"I am waiting to take a ride in the Piper Cub." I showed him my five bucks.

"You have to be accompanied by an adult. Are your parents here?"

"The notice said fourteen and under has to be accompanied. I am fifteen and a half."

He looked at me up and down. "Don't lie to me boy. You are not over thirteen if you're that. Get out of line."

"I *am* fifteen and a half, my birthday was in December." He grabbed me by the collar. "Hey! Stop! Let go!" He dragged me out of line.

"Your parents need to wash your mouth out with soap for lying. Anyone can see that you are not fifteen. Move along and don't come back."

"But I *am fifteen*. Honest. Come on mister. I'm old enough and I have the money."

He made a threatening move and I backed away. "Go! Git you lying little troublemaker." Several people in line shook their heads but did not say anything. I did not know if they agreed with him or were sympathetic to me. I walked away.

I leaned on a barrier at the edge of the airfield, watching the people get in line for the Piper Cub. After several minutes, the guard yelled at me. "Hey kid! Are you still here? I told you to get lost!"

"Ah come on mister, I'm just watching. Ain't I old enough to watch?"

He started toward me. "I told you to git, boy. There's no loitering around the planes. These ain't amusement park rides."

I backed away from the fence protesting. "I ain't hurting your darned old planes."

I moved away from the fence but kept my eye on the guard. When he turned his back, I slipped around the side of a building and walked along the fence, frustrated. I came to an open gate.

I did not see anyone around, and I slipped through the gate. I cautiously approached the open hangar, looked inside and caught my breath. Just a few feet away sat a Stearman PT-17 in navy colors just like the ones in Dad's manuals. I looked around the hangar and did not see anyone. I skulked inside and then, throwing caution to the wind, I boldly walked across the hangar to the airplane. I looked around and climbed onto the wing, carefully walking on the wing walk.

I learned many of the instruments and controls from the manuals and I became engrossed in staring at the cockpit and dreaming of being at the controls.

"Hey boy! What are you doing there?"

I jumped and banged my head on the upper wing and went down on my backside. I scrambled off the wing, holding my head.

A tall, rugged man wearing red coveralls was coming from outside accompanied by an Asian fellow. The man's coveralls had a patch that matched the insignia on the side of the airplane and his name patch named him Daniel Kelly. He stuffed a pair of aviator's sunglasses in his breast pocket.

"I asked what you were doing in here, boy."

"I wasn't doing anything. Just looking. Honest. I didn't touch anything."

"You didn't touch anything?" He scoffed. "You were crawling all over my airplane, boy. Standing on the wing, poking in the cockpit."

"I was just looking, mister. Honest. I came from the park. A sign there, on the board, said I could go for a ride for five dollars."

"You're in the wrong place." His tone mellowed. "The flight school is where you want to be. Two buildings down." He gestured toward the flight line.

"I was there, but they wouldn't believe that I am fifteen."

"Are you fifteen?" He looked skeptical. "You're a bit small."

"Yeah." I shook my head feeling suddenly frustrated. "Yeah, I am. I can't help it if I'm small. Not everyone is tall." I kicked at an imaginary rock. "That's just one more reason I can't be a pilot. I wear glasses. *You're too small... blah... blah... blah.* I hear that all the time. Shoot!" I waved my hand in disgust, hung my head, and turned to walk away.

"Hey boy, I didn't say you could leave. What's your name?" The man's commanding voice stopped me.

"Michael."

"Well Michael. You are *not* too small and there's no reason you can't fly wearing glasses. Do you want to go for a ride?" Kelly nodded at the biplane.

I could not believe my ears. Is he kidding? I did not hesitate. "In the Stearman? Yeah, for sure!"

"My name is Kelly. Dan Kelly and this is my plane." He offered his hand. "I think I can arrange a little ride."

He offered his hand, and I shook it.

"Mister Kelly. Thank you."

"You wait here and don't touch anything."

He started toward the office but turned and pointed at me. "Don't touch anything, you hear?" He grinned roguishly.

"Yeah, I hear." I grinned and stuffed my hands in my pockets. "See. I ain't touching nothing."

Kelly laughed.

The Asian fellow introduced himself. "Hello. I am Kim Jung, Mister Kelly's mechanic." He grinned broadly. I smiled and shook his hand. He was not much taller than me. His accent was heavy, his grammar broken, but he was understandable.

"Come. You help Kim check airplane." I followed him as he checked the plane over. He described each procedure. I helped him push it to the fuel pump.

I tried to make conversation. "Have you worked for Mr. Kelly very long, Mr. Jung?"

"You call me Kim. Kim comes to America in the last three years, with Daniel Kelly."

"Are you from China?" From the look on Kim's face, I knew I had said something wrong.

"Kim from Korea."

"Oh, I'm sorry I didn't mean to…"

"Is Ok. Kim understands." He brightened and smiled, "We all look same to you. Kim understands. You all look same to Kim, too." I laughed and he spoke. "Come. Mr. Kelly is back. We push plane to tarmac."

"Your English is pretty good."

"Kim learns some from American pilots during war. But I have much to learn. Kim's children are going to school, and they speak better than father. Wife also better." He grinned.

Kelly came and did his pre-flight inspection, giving me a running commentary, interspersed with the occasional joke, on what he was doing and why. Kelly had an easy going manner about him. Kim helped me fasten the three-point shoulder harness, as Kelly got in the rear cockpit. He told me to keep my hands clear of the controls… to keep them on my knees. He took his time describing the controls and their function. I listened intently and enjoyed every moment, anticipating the take-off.

We were ready and he called *"Clear"* as Kim stood by with a fire extinguisher. The roar of the engine was as rousing as I had imagined, and it set my heart pumping.

We taxied to the end of the runway and moved into position after one plane touched down. Kelly waited until the airplane turned off the runway and then he opened the throttle. The roar of the engine rose to a deafening crescendo and the plane surged forward. The plane raced down the runway, the engine throbbing in my head and making my heart pound in my chest… trying to keep time with the engine. The plane leaped into the air, and I was pressed back into the seat. My stomach rumbled and I fought back a sick feeling as Kelly climbed steeply, not quite vertical. I was afraid my first flight was going to turn into a disaster, but I managed to keep my stomach under control.

The airfield fell away and then the world turned on its side as Kelly banked sharply away from the airport. I was looking straight down at the park and the lake below. The experience was scary and stimulating. It was a lot different from the Allegheny Airlines I rode in when I flew to Erie to visit cousins last summer.

We flew away to the west toward the Blue Ridge Mountains. My adrenaline was in a rush as Kelly performed banks and turns, explaining each maneuver.

My stomach had butterflies and my heart throbbed when Kelly told me to take the controls. He talked me through level turns, showing me how to hold my altitude as we turned. We used a straight part of highway below as a guide. I could barely hold my excitement and after a rough start I overcame my excitement and nervousness to make several good turns. Kelly encouraged me, "That's very good, Michael."

"Wow! This is great!"

"Relax. I have the controls." I let go of the stick and kept my feet clear of the rudder bar.

My heart was back to normal, but after a lazy eight and a chandelle, it was racing again and an Immelman got my stomach tumbling again. We climbed straight up, entered a loop and at the top rolled from inverted to level flight.

Kelly led me through a climbing turn, more complicated than a level turn. I overcame my nerves after several tries and climbed smoothly a thousand feet in a turn and leveled off at the correct altitude on the opposite heading. I felt like I was in heaven… and I forgot the time.

"Let's try some real flying." Kelly took control. He did a barrel roll followed by a snap roll and I thought I was going to lose my lunch. I managed a weak, "Yaahooo!" I wanted to learn to fly more than ever.

"Are you ok?"

"Yeah. This is great!"

"You liked that? How about this?" He began a loop, rolled to level flight, started an inside loop and after a steep dive returned to level flight, finishing with snap rolls.

I felt queasy. "Oh god!" I covered my mouth expecting to barf.

"You ok? Want to quit?" Kelly laughed.

"N-No. I'm ok." I lied. I was about to up-chuck.

Kelly said. "If you feel sick, there is a bag in the pocket on the left… use that." I used it. "We better get you back. What time is your bus leaving?"

"Oh my God, I forgot." I checked my watch. "Mister Lockhart will be really mad."

"What time?" Kelly repeated.

"Four o'clock."

"Ok, we'll do one more and then go back." He pulled up, let the airplane stall, and forced it into a spin. As the plane spiraled earthward, I grabbed hold of the sides of the cockpit and for a moment relived the dream from this morning. Kelly brought it out of the spin easily, but I got sick again and missed the bag.

"Oh, yuk!... Eew!" I moaned. Jeez I didn't get sick this morning… but that was a dream… this is real.

"Uh-Oh. You didn't get sick, did you?"

"Yeah. I missed the bag. Sorry." I was embarrassed.

Kelly laughed. "That's ok. It happens. We will get back and get you cleaned up, after we do one more thing."

"Oh God no, not another…"

"This will be easy, it's called landing."

"Oh. I think I can manage that."

We approached the airport and Kelly gave a running description of the procedure. The landing was smooth. After a second demonstration, he let me take the controls and he talked me through it as he kept his hand lightly on the controls. I came in a little high the first time. He took control as we went around. The second time went smoother, and I made a good approach but landed hard and bounced a couple of times. Kelly laughed as he accelerated and went around again. The third time I made a smooth landing; touched down on the main wheels and let the tail settle.

"Very good, Michael you have a knack for flying." The mess on my pants did not dampen my enthusiasm. Kelly helped me clean up while Kim cleaned the plane. Kim drove me back to the park in an old Jeep.

As we pulled into the parking lot, Mister Lockhart rushed from the bus as I jumped out of the Jeep.

CHAPTER 4

"*Michael!* Where the devil have you been? I've been worried about you." Mister Lockhart growled. "I thought you had passed out somewhere or fallen in the canal."

"I was over at the airpark. I went flying…"

"You should not have left the park." He grasped my collar and hauled me toward the bus. "Get on the bus… now!"

As I got on the bus the other students began yelling, "Where were you, Michael? Did you get lost in the restroom?"

"I went flying at the airpark and…"

John called out. "I knew it! You fell asleep on the toilet and were dreaming again." He laughed. "I guess I hit you harder than I thought. Knocked you right into never-never land." Everyone laughed.

"No. I really was flying." I insisted. "There was a…" I was cut off by jeers and laughter.

"Sit down Michael. You're daydreaming again." Dennis Spiers poked me.

John kept up his rant. "You scrawny little wimp, who would be foolish enough to let you near an airplane? How would you see over the dash?" He looked at the departing Jeep and sneered. "Hey, who's your chink friend?"

"Don't call people names, jerk. He's not a chink, he's Korean," I snapped. "What are you? Some kind of bigot?"

"Looks like a commie to me. You a commie lover?" John prodded. The other kids became quiet.

"McCaskey! Shut up!" Lockhart came along the aisle and pointed at the big teenager, "I don't want to hear your garbage."

"He can't help..." I stopped at Lockhart's hard look. He was not smiling.

"Sit, and be quiet, Michael. You've caused enough trouble today. No more nonsense. You're only making trouble for yourself with your stories."

"It's not a story..." At Lockhart's angry look, I shut up and sat down. Lockhart let his gaze wander over the busload of students. Everyone was quiet. He glared at John. The big teenager hunkered down in his seat.

Lockhart returned to the front of the bus, looked around and motioned the driver to go; then he sat down. No one spoke for a long time. I could feel the other students looking at me. I was frustrated that no one would believe me, especially Dennis, my friend. I did not think it was *my* fault even though I *did* have a reputation for daydreaming in class.

John looked at the back of Lockhart's head and then over the back of his seat at me and formed the words, *"four eyes."* I stared at him but did not respond. John pressed on; he formed the words, *"Commie lover."*

I raised my fist and displayed my middle finger and heard a familiar female voice whisper. *"Michael!"* I saw Connie duck her head. She stared straight ahead, covering her face with a hand.

I bit my lip and tried to hide my hand under my coat. I slouched down in the seat and pulled my cap down over my face. I wanted to disappear.

I chanced a peek at Connie. She was peeking at me out of the corner of her eye. She was trying to stifle a giggle. Darn, she probably thinks I'm silly and stupid. I remembered her kiss and closed my eyes. I've probably blown it with her, not that I ever had a chance.

As the bus bounced along the driveway, I leaned back in the seat, closed my eyes, and relived the flight… and the kiss.

Mister Lockhart came back and asked me to come and sit with him. I thought maybe he had seen me make the rude gesture. I glanced at Connie; she was biting her lip, her eyes wide.

"You should not have gone off by yourself, Michael." Lockhart admonished me after we sat down.

"I'm sorry, Mr. Lockhart, but you said I could hang around the park, or the zoo and I thought the airpark was part of the park?"

Lockhart let out a sigh and a chuckle. "That's slicing hairs, but I guess you're right. But… you should have let me know where you were going. You had me worried. After that hit you took, I was afraid you might have passed out somewhere. I should have taken you to the first aid center. You kids are my responsibility and if anything happens to you… I don't want anything to happen to any of you."

I spoke. "I'm sorry. I know I should have told you where I was going. I just got excited when I saw the ad on the board about an introductory flight for five dollars and I had enough money. I thought this is my chance to make my dreams a reality." I snorted a sardonic laugh. "But they wouldn't believe I was fifteen…"

"Yeah, yeah, Mikey, tell us about your fantasies, and flying with the chink. Commie lover…" John sneered.

"Kim is a Korean veteran you…" I did not get a chance to finish as Lockhart put a hand on my shoulder and shot out of his seat. He was standing over John. His face was a livid; his finger was in John's face, barely touching his nose. "You listen to me John and listen well. I don't want to hear any more of your bullshit." The students gasped. In spite of his rough veneer, Mr. Lockhart never swore in front of the kids. The bus went eerily silent. "I fought a war because of tyrants and bigots. I will not put up with it in my hearing. If I hear one more peep out of you, I might forget you are a student.

"Maybe you like to bully people who are smaller than you." John's face showed fear and terror as Lockhart's finger jabbed his chest. "I do not like bullies. You should know that by now. Do you understand me, boy?"

"Y… y… yes sir, Mr. Lockhart! I understand." The big student seemed to shrink with each word. Lockhart laid his open hand on John's chest and grinned.

"Good." John winced at Lockhart's rage. "You get back to the rear of the bus. I do not want you sitting behind me, listening where you have no business. Move. Now!" John hurried back.

I was silent after Lockhart returned to his seat; everyone was unnaturally quiet.

Mr. Lockhart spoke quietly. "What *is* it between you and that boy, Michael? It can't just be bullying."

I kept my reply quiet. "He tried to steal my bike last year and my brother, Andy, knocked him on his as… uh, butt." I looked warily at Mister Lockhart. "When my brother turned his back John hit him with a rock and then my cousin Doug jumped on John and broke his nose… I think… it was awfully bloody." Lockhart was chuckling. "What?" I asked.

"So, that was you boys in River Park last year. Everyone thinks it was some gang from Harrisburg."

"We thought it was better not to talk about it. I didn't think anyone would believe us anyway, and we got in trouble with Mom and Dad."

Lockhart chuckled. "The township council has been discussing Mac and his gang. They make trouble all over the county. It is a good idea to stay out of their way."

I laughed quietly. "Yeah, I can't fight worth a darn. We were lucky in River Park. I don't think I'd get that lucky again. Believe me we do not go looking for them."

"Fighting's not as much fun as John Wayne makes it appear."

"Maybe, but it's more fun not getting your teeth knocked out; or your head busted."

He laughed.

When I got home Mister Lockhart talked to Dad and we had a family meeting after dinner that night.

"I couldn't go swimming because of getting knocked out in the ball game. I was dizzy and Mr. Lockhart said it was ok if I skipped the swimming. He said I could hang around…"

"Knocked out! Lockhart didn't say anything about you getting knocked out." Mom looked at Dad, her fists on her hips. "Did Mister Lockhart tell you Michael got knocked out, James?" She did not wait for a reply. "How did you get knocked out?"

"Whoa! Easy, Mom. I wasn't *really* knocked out, just sort of dazed. John McCaskey ran into me at home plate…"

"McCaskey!" She cried, "I knew we shouldn't have let him go to that park with that ruffian." She gave Dad a prickly look. "And where was Mister Lockhart during this brawl?"

"It wasn't a brawl, Mom. Take it easy. It was just a game and Mister Lockhart was umping." She glared at me.

"Don't tell me to *take it easy*, young man. What do you mean he was *umping*?" She barked. "Why…" Dad interrupted.

"Anne, calm down. Michael was not hurt. Let him explain before you go crazy."

She retorted, "I am not going *crazy*."

"Why did John run into you?" Dad asked.

"We were playing baseball, and I was catching. John was trying to beat the throw home and I was blocking the plate. He ran into me."

Dad's eyes narrowed. "Did you catch the ball?"

Mom scowled and muttered, barely audible, "What?"

"Yeah, but I dropped it when he hit me."

Dad made a pained look, "Damn."

I hastily added, "He fell over me and missed the plate. I was laying on the ball… and the plate. When he tried to touch the plate, I tagged him. Lockhart called him out. Boy was he ever mad… he went nuts." I laughed.

Dad grinned and pumped his fist. "Yes!" Dad was an avid baseball fan

Mom's mouth hung open. "*Hey!* Let's stick to the point here. That ruffian knocked out your son and you're cheering?"

"Anne, it was an accident." Dad tried to explain. "It's part of the game. It happens."

"It happens? I didn't know tackling was a part of baseball."

"Come on, Mom, it wasn't a tackle, and I wasn't hurt… just shook up. I just had to sit and rest until I got my bearings. Mister Lockhart didn't want me to lie down."

"Well. I do not like it. That McCaskey boy is dangerous. He probably hit you hard on purpose. I don't like you hanging around him."

"I don't hang around him." I groaned. "We go to the same school and school is out for the summer, so you don't have to worry."

When I told them about flying with Mister Kelly and about his suggestion that I take flying lessons they became less forthcoming.

"You are dreaming, Michael… again. You don't have time for that." Dad argued.

"You're rushing things. You're too young. You're trying to grow up too quickly. You will have plenty of time for that when you finish school." Mom warned. "You need to spend time with the kids from the church." Dad did not say anything.

"I was not dreaming, Dad. I went flying and Mister Kelly said I was good. It won't take that much time only a couple of hours on the weekend."

"We can't afford it, Michael." Dad said.

"I have money in my savings account, and I can earn more. It won't cost that much to start. Ten or fifteen dollars a class."

Dad was not enthusiastic. "We will talk about it later. You have to finish summer school. You start that on Monday so get ready. You are going to be doing a lot of studying and you will *not* have time for anything else. And don't forget we are going to the national matches in July, so you are going to be very busy for the next two months... and have you given up on sailing? Your summer is pretty well planned. So, you can just let it go for now."

I had forgotten all of that in my excitement. Andy, Charlie and I had been really looking forward to going to the CMP/NRA National Shooting matches in Camp Perry. I wondered when... or if I would have time for flying... and I did want to learn to sail in my boat.

CHAPTER 5

I sat in the cafeteria, looking out the window, watching kids playing on the field behind the high school. I was sitting at the staff table at the back of the cafeteria trying to study algebra and ignore the hubbub around me. Many kids were attending summer school from outside the district, so it was more crowded than I expected. I was daydreaming again, looking at the bright sunlit day and thinking about sailing.

I built a boat in our garage at home during the winter and I was eager to try sailing it. I had rowed it around near the east shore earlier in the spring but then decided to put a sail on it. I read books and magazines on sailing and made a sail… with my mom helping me… or rather doing all the work while I watched. She was a professional seamstress. I set up the mast and rigged it. I wanted to test my knowledge.

An airplane flew by headed for Harrisburg and broke my reverie. I sighed and turned to the books in front of me. "Algebra." I muttered. "What good is this stuff anyway?"

I was forced to adapt to the intense study schedule because I had a test coming up. Quick tests were given every day; big tests came on Fridays. I needed to review my notes and books quietly. I tried to concentrate.

"May I sit here?" I did not respond at once. I was not sure the girl's request was directed at me; however, no one else was nearby and she repeated her question.

I looked into the prettiest brown eyes. The girl's straight black hair hung to her shoulders and long bangs framed a brown face. She wore a knee length plaid skirt, a white long sleeved blouse with lace at the collar and cuffs. A string of pearls encircled the high collar.

My very first thought was *she's cute*. I wondered why I had never thought Negro girls were pretty before. I was staring and she looked at me oddly. I blurted. "What? Oh, I'm sorry I wasn't paying attention." I laughed and fidgeted.

She ducked her head and suggested, "I can sit somewhere else."

"Oh, no. I mean yes… you can sit here. It's fine with me. I was just concentrating on this, uh… algebra." I grimaced.

"I'm Katherine Meirs. My friends call me Kathy." She extended her hand, and I shook it gently. Her firm grip belied her shy persona. She set her book bag on the floor, put a bottle of coke on the table, and sat a couple of chairs away. "I've seen you around York Landing."

"I'm Michael Hunter." I replied brightly with a shrug. "Yeh, I hang around by the river. I have a new boat I want to try out soon with a sail."

"Michael? May I call you Mike?"

"I guess I'm not a Mike kind of guy. Mike is like…" I made like a muscle man, flexing my arms and hunching my shoulders, and talking huskily, "Me, Mike, ooh, ooh. Strong like Bull." She laughed pleasantly. "Everyone calls me Michael. My mother insists that she named me Michael and she would like everyone to call me Michael." I was babbling and shrugged self-consciously. She showed a mouthful of beautiful white teeth when she laughed. Her laugh was cute, reminding me of the sound of water falling over stones in a brook near home.

"So, I will not offend your mother. Michael it is. What are you here for?" She smiled cheerily. "Did you say Algebra?"

"Yeah. I failed Algebra One. What about you? What's your offense?"

"I'm taking courses for extra credit."

"You're here because you *want* to be? Now I've heard everything. The whole summer in front of you and you're wasting it here?"

"I like studying. It's not a waste. I get extra credits for college."

"I guess I should admire you. If I had my choice, which I don't," I shrugged, "I'd be taking flying lessons. But alas, here I am stuck taking Algebra."

"I love algebra. Working with formulas is fun."

Facetiously I asked, "Formulas is fun?" and I reflected a moment looking at her. "Uh… uh… No. I'm not going there." I grimaced.

"What?" She looked wary. "Not going where?"

I chuckled. "I was going to suggest if you like doing algebra so much maybe you could do mine for me."

"Oh, I would be glad to *help* you. It will give me practice."

"Practice?"

"Yes. I am going to be a teacher." She announced proudly.

"I was joking. That *would* be a waste of your time trying to teach me. And you have your own studies."

"Ah-hah. Now that sounds like a challenge." She moved closer and leaned over to look at my work. "What are you working on?" She barely touched me but the heat from her body and her fragrance filled my senses, and her face close to mine sent my blood racing and my heart beating. She looked at the papers, but I was looking at her smooth, soft brown skin and dainty upturned nose. She was mere inches from my face. I wondered what it would be like to kiss her. The feeling was exhilarating and more than a little uncomfortable. I shook my head, averted my gaze and tried to focus on the papers in front of us.

I mumbled, cleared my throat, and tried to speak clearly, protesting weakly. "You sure you want to? I'd hate to take up your time." After some gentle prodding from her, I relented. I liked being near her and I could not help wondering if it was right for me to feel this way with all the race problems in the news.

Inter-racial relationships were frowned on by many people though I think it was more of an adult thing. The kids at school did not seem to pay a lot of attention to such things, at least in our class. I recalled there were problems in some larger cities. I began to wonder about such things for the first time in my short life. Kathy is a pretty girl and obviously as nice as any other girl. It was an awakening; I had never thought of such things in spite of the daily news.

"Show me what you're working on." she demanded.

With some difficulty, I described my dilemma, and she quickly found my problem. She seemed to be oblivious of her effect on me and I forced myself to concentrate on the book.

Summer school was six weeks of intense class work, two classes a day with a study period of one hour between classes. Thanks to Kathy's help, my grades went up, to my parents delight. I did not tell them about Kathy. I don't know why. Maybe I thought they would disapprove.

It occurred to me the fear was silly, as Dad was on the race relations board in the township and Mom worked with women of different nationalities and races at the naval base tailor shop. She often had them over to the house. Mom was a skilled tailor and was delighted to share her knowledge with others. The laughter and delightful babble filled the house as they shared tea and pastries. They talked about religion a lot and I usually stayed out of the way, working in my hobby shop in the basement.

Kathy and I kept a study relationship; however, I looked forward to being with her. My affection for her was growing. She was gracious, funny, and intelligent; a hard persistent taskmaster. She showed an intense interest in me and my dreams… when we weren't concentrating on class work. I learned that Kathy would be in my class the coming year.

I was holding the door of the cafeteria for Kathy, when a group of older boys pushed through, bumped into her and knocked her books loose. I jumped to help catch her books. I yelled at the ruffians. "Hey watch out! You almost ran over us… jeez! What a bunch of jerks."

"Are you calling me a jerk, boy?" One of the bigger boys stopped. "I'll teach you and your darky friend your place. Whites come first; blacks go to the back of the line."

"That's crap. Black people have the same rights as everyone else. You are stupid." I was wary but I stood up and faced him. I abhorred bullies and it occurred to me that racism was another form of bullying.

"If anyone belongs at the back of the line its ignorant jerks like you." I faced the thug defiantly. He made a threatening move toward me.

Kathy grabbed my sleeve. "Michael!" She tugged at me. "Please don't. Let's just go."

"He shouldn't talk about you like that…"

"You better listen to your n…"

"Pardon me!" A school attendant interrupted him before he could complete his vulgar rant. *"You."* He addressed the thug. "We do not tolerate that kind of talk here. One more word and you will be out the door." The attendant turned on me. "We do not tolerate fighting here, either. If you have a problem, take it to the office. Fighting will get you expelled… *understand?* Now move along, *all* of you. You are blocking the door."

The attendant moved off, shooing the thugs ahead of him. Kathy and I were silent as we found our table.

"Would you like a coke?" I offered.

"Maybe you shouldn't hang around with me." She looked worried.

"Why not? Because of what that jerk said. People shouldn't talk like that. And you should not have to put up with it." The intensity of my feelings warmed my face. "I have had to deal with bullies before."

"That is not the first time, Michael, and probably will not be the last. I don't want you to get into trouble because of me." She bit her lip and asked warily. "If we were not friends, Michael, would you have… come to my defense?"

Disturbed by the question, I looked around the cafeteria and I did not like the conclusion I came to. "No, probably not. I would have done the same as everyone else." People were going about their business as if nothing had happened. "I would have looked the other way." I felt shame.

She touched my arm. "The truth is most people, black or white, would have looked the other way. People just don't want to get involved."

"That doesn't make it right." I spoke. "I like you. If people think I'm your, uh… boyfriend." My face got warm. "Well, that's fine with me." She looked around. "Being around you has been nice. For more than just the algebra." I let out a breath. "I like you. You are a friend and I hope you consider me your friend."

"I *am* your friend and I like you, and I like being with you, too." She studied her hands awkwardly. "But you know we can only be just friends, not… uh… boyfriend-girlfriend like? I don't want to get you in trouble."

I exhaled. "I guess, but I don't have to like it that we can't be together because it might offend someone." I scoffed and laughed. "I don't do dating anyway, so there's probably not much danger there." I thought for a second. "*You* are worth getting in trouble over." My face became warmer. My emotions were entering new territory. I babbled. "You can't leave me now. I'm about to pass algebra and it's because of your help. You are a good teacher. I envy your future students."

She smiled. "I guess I'm no Rosa Parks. I'm not brave enough to make waves."

"Rosa Parks? Oh. *Oh!* Yeah. The Black lady… down south? She got into trouble over a bus seat." I was quiet. "I guess we don't think about those problems around here. They seem to be so far away, as if they don't affect us."

"They're really not that far away."

I glanced at the door. "Yeah, I guess not." I smiled. "Anyway, aren't you going with Pete?" Pete Simon was a basketball player in our class.

Her eyes went wide, and she blushed. "Pete? Oh. No. not really… I mean I like him… we go to the same church, and we hang around a little, but we aren't together." She paused and made a sly smile, looking out of the corner of her eye. "At least not yet."

We laughed and I wondered. "Maybe I should warn Pete."

She smacked my arm. *"Don't you dare."* She looked around warily.

The end of summer school came too quickly, and I had mixed feelings, happy that it was done, but sad that I would not see Kathy for the rest of the summer. We met in a park off campus near the school. She was waiting on a bench by herself when I ran up. She jumped up when she saw me. "How did you do? How did you do, Michael? Tell me!"

I threw my arms around her. "I got a ninety-six on the final! I've never gotten over eighty in math."

"Yay!" She hugged me tightly and we jumped excitedly. *"Wow, Michael! That's great!"* I picked her up and whirled her around. I kissed her on the cheek and then we kissed passionately. When I put her down, she stepped back giggling and smoothing her dress and looking around.

She had a delightful pink hue to her brown complexion. The kiss was spontaneous, and it was exhilarating, if embarrassing.

"Well." She cleared her throat and folded her arms across her stomach. "I guess that is it for the summer."

"Yeah, I guess." We sat down on the bench and talked for a while about the summer. I think neither of us wanted the moment to end too soon. We shared a hug and a long kiss before we parted. She left me breathing heavily and hungry for more. I sat down for a little while savoring the moment. I think I like kissing girls even if it does leave me with shaky knees.

CHAPTER 6

We were planning to leave the next day for Ohio and the National Rifle matches at Camp Perry but as I pedaled home, I was thinking about flying. It was just after noon when I arrived at Old York Road. Harrisburg State Airport was just 3 miles up the road, an easy bike ride. Having all afternoon, I headed up the road to the airport.

I found the flight school and wandered around the pilot's lounge looking at pictures of students and pilots, many featuring Daniel Kelly.

Mister Kelly came from the office and saw me. "Michael, what are you doing here?"

"I came from summer school. I was wondering about taking flying lessons."

"If I remember, you were fifteen. You will not be eligible to get a student license until you are sixteen."

"Oh." I stuffed my hands in my pockets and looked around. "I am sixteen in December, isn't there something I can do until then? Even if I can't fly yet?"

"Hmmm. I suppose you could take an introductory flight. Do you have five dollars?"

I fumbled in my pocket and produced four dollars and a handful of change. It added up to five dollars and seventy-five-cents. "Yeah. I can do that."

"I don't want to take all your money."

"I have more… at home."

"Ok we'll take the Grasshopper."

"What is a Grasshopper?"

He laughed. "It's a Piper Cub in war paint. Cubs were used in the war for observation and utility transport. Some General called the Cub a Grasshopper and it stuck."

We flew around for a half-an-hour and Kelly let me do a few touch and go landings, bouncing the plane just one time.

"You do very well, Michael. You could probably solo very quickly… once you have your license." He scratched his chin, thinking. "There is no reason you can't take ground school classes. But can you afford it?"

"Oh Yeah." I answered excitedly… without thinking about it.

Before I left the airport, I saw Kim and we talked about working on motors; he was interested in my work at Dietrich's, and he asked if I would like to learn about airplane engines. He said I could come for a few hours in the shop after ground school and he would teach me about airplane motors. Dad was an aircraft mechanic in the war; I was sure he would like that.

As I rode home, I was thinking hard about how I would pay for the lessons. I almost ran off the road and just missed hitting a tractor on the country road.

I thought I would have to dip into my savings. I have saved my allowance and with the small income I receive from working part time at Dietrich's Marine Service, cleaning the floors and tools and working on outboard engines; I can do it… I was certain… I hoped.

I planned to sign up for the classes in August after Ohio, but now I needed to find more work. I thought of the farms near home; they hired students during the summer and there was one right across the road from my home.

"So, you're going to sneak over to the airfield to take flying lessons… without permission." Dad said.

"I was not sneaking, Dad. I went to the airport after school. I had all afternoon, and I did not see why I had to be home early."

"Mister Kelly said I can take the ground school on weekends. I can't fly yet… until I'm sixteen. Kim said he could teach me airplane mechanics."

"So, you *are* thinking about getting into aircraft mechanics." Dad seemed to like that.

"Yeah, it looks like it will be interesting. I have been working on motors at Dietrich's. It will be kind of like what Kathy was doing at summer school, getting advanced schooling."

"Who is Kathy?" Mom and Dad asked simultaneously.

"Oh. Uh, just a girl at summer school who helped me with algebra. Kathy Meirs. She was taking extra courses to prepare for teacher's college."

"That is Jennie's daughter. That was nice of her… to help you."

"So, you want to spend your summer in a classroom." Dad laughed. "This I have to see."

"It will only be for an hour or so on weekends and not every day. I will have plenty of time for other things like sailing and scouting." I spoke. "So, I can do it?"

"I did not say that." Dad retorted. "How are you going to pay for this?"

"It's just a few bucks. I can take it from my savings and maybe I can work on the farms around here."

"It's your money Michael, but I think it is a waste of time. I think you'll lose interest." Dad said. "I think you are biting off more than you can chew; flying, sailing and scouts? Not to mention all the work you are going to have to do. Your summer will be gone before you know it, and what about Ohio? We leave first thing in the morning. It's a long drive. Or aren't you going to that now?"

"Yes." Mom said. "Get your stuff together and pack your bag. I will check to see that you haven't forgotten anything."

Dad added with a laugh. "And don't forget your rifle. We will buy ammo there."

"Why would I forget that?"

"Your mind is on so many things, you might forget your head if it weren't screwed on." He chuckled.

Mom said. "I am glad you are taking an interest in these things, Michael but I wish you would take more interest in your faith. You should not neglect that."

"Oh, here we go again." Dad muttered. "Do you have to start on that now?"

"It is important, James; more important than flying or rifles… or material possessions. You can gain all the *things* in the world, and you will not be happy unless you have a relationship with God and his son Jesus Christ."

Dad scoffed and left for the legion.

I went to get my stuff together and Mom began playing hymns on the old piano. I always enjoyed her playing. She was talented though she never took lessons.

After a few hymns, I asked. "Why do you and dad argue over the church?"

She looked sad. "I'm sorry we argue so in front of you boys. One would never believe that your father and I met at a church social." She smiled and looked thoughtful. "Your father was quite shy. He played on church baseball teams in the valley." She sighed, "I don't know what happened to him in the war, but he seems to have less respect for the church or religion and less time for God. He sees too much hypocrisy in the church. They make him angry because they seem to oppose him on everything in the township, especially things to do with kids."

I spoke. "Church doesn't seem to do them any good. It only seems to get in the way when Dad wants to get something done. I don't see how the church, or God, can help me."

"Unfortunately, the men… or women… of the church are not always the best testimony to God. The church's leaders are men, and they have their flaws… no less or no more than any of us."

"But we should trust in the Lord, not in men. It is so important, Michael. We can get caught up in life and forget there is much more. Faith is not just 'pie-in-the-sky-by-and-by'. Jesus can help us in the here and now. We need to trust him every day."

"Proverbs three, five-six says 'Trust in the Lord with all your heart. Do not lean on your own understanding. In all your ways acknowledge him and he will direct your paths'. Jesus warns us not to lay up treasures on earth where they can rust and rot. But we are encouraged to lay up treasures in heaven. It's good to make plans for the future but it is important to include God in your plans."

The summer flew by; we attended the nationals… and we all did well. After we came home, I made the trek to the airport once a week attending ground school on Saturday mornings and working with Kim in the shop in the afternoon. I found time during the week for sailing and the scouts between doing odd jobs on farms near home.

I needed better transportation… especially with winter coming up and I bought an old army surplus scooter from the nearby army depot. I began to clean it up at Dietrich's shop. I was very busy and sometimes it seemed like there were not enough hours in a day… or a week, which my mother seldom failed to remind me.

CHAPTER 7

Labor Day came too soon and the end of summer and school loomed. I left home Saturday morning on my bike bound for the airport. I rode along Valley Rd making good time and working up a sweat in the late summer heat. Rain the night before added to the humidity.

I glanced in the mirror to see the Pontiac crest a rise behind me. It was moving fast, fishtailing all over the wet road every time it hit a bump.

I moved onto the shoulder to let the car go past. The Pontiac's rear end hit the shoulder and the car careened right at me. I dived into the water-filled ditch as the car careened past chewing up the narrow shoulder. The car screeched to a stop and backed up as I climbed out of the ditch, my pants soaked. *"Great!"*

"Hey, boy, you alright?" The driver shouted… it was Jimmie McCaskey, John's big brother, though he was not as big as John… at least not as tall. Warning bells were going off in my head and I hoped he did not recognize me. During that infamous brawl last year I broke his arm with a two by four… that's when the fight ended, when he ran off followed by his gang.

Luckily, Mom insisted I wear the old aviator's helmet and goggles. She thought they would protect me if I fell, but they made a good disguise.

"Yeah, no thanks to you. You're gonna kill someone driving like that."

Jimmie was medium height, in a sleeveless black leather vest and a sleeveless T-shirt that displayed his well-muscled arms. His black hair was swept back in a ducktail. He had a much better build than the summer before on River Road. What a difference a year makes. Mac… known as Mac the Hammer… was notorious for knocking guys out with one punch. He swaggered toward me.

"You don't like my driving, boy?"

"You need to be careful is all I am saying. There are kids living along this road."

"There is nothing but farm animals out here. These roads are for cars. You ride them at your own peril."

I scoffed. "This is a public road and farm kids are always riding here. You need to slow down. This is not a race track."

"You have a smart mouth for such a runt." He started back to his car.

I began to clean the mud from the bike chain. "I'm just pointing out the truth. I'm not trying to be smart."

He turned and spoke. "What did you say, boy? You got something to say, say it to my face."

Uh-oh. "I didn't say anything." I got on my bike ready to take off in a hurry, but he was too quick, and he pushed me off the bike into the ditch again. My temper soared and I jumped up yelling. "I did not say anything to you, you bast—" I saw his shoulder twitch and I turned my head slightly as his fist struck the side of the leather helmet.

I fell into the water again, only slightly dazed thanks to the helmet; the water helped. He walked back to his car laughing. My anger seething, I bounded from the ditch, threw caution to the wind, and ran up behind him. I pushed him into his car and slammed his face down onto the trunk lid. He tried to turn but I grabbed his vest and shirt and pulled them over his head, spun him around, kicked him in the backside and pushed him into the water- filled ditch on the other side of the road.

I ran to his car, set the gear shift in neutral, released the hand brake and ran for my bike as he struggled out of the ditch, all wet and cursing a blue streak. He started after me but then saw his car rolling away and ran after it. I pedaled furiously, heading back up the road toward home. I was scolding myself for inciting him more. I should have just let him go. Mom and Dad were always warning me about my temper.

But now, I needed to get out of Mac's sight fast; I just *knew* he would come after me. I glanced back and saw the car roll into the ditch and stop. I passed over a slight rise and rounded a bend. I heard the squeal of his tires behind me and looked for a way off the road. However, the roadside embankments were too high. The car was still out of sight when I came to the Kessler's Feed Store, turned in, and hid behind a shed. I did not have to wait long. The Pontiac roared past kicking up a cloud of dust and disappeared around a bend. I headed back down the road toward the airport, pedaling as fast as my tired legs could take me. I did not doubt that Mac would come back to the feed store as soon as he realized I was not in front of him.

I pedaled hard for a long time and turned onto Old York Road before tiring and easing up. The dunk in the water had cooled me for a spell but I was getting hot again. I was heading down Old York Road and he had not appeared; I was sure I had lost him. I entered a long serpentine downhill section approaching the turnpike overpass. I heard horns sounding behind me and glanced behind to see that bloody Pontiac roar into sight around a bend and almost run another car off the road.

I began pedaling madly looking for a way off the road. There were some driveways but the only turnoffs along this section were near the bottom where two roads entered at a sharp angle. I doubted that I could make those turns.

The race of my life was on, and I was so frantic I nearly lost control as I took curves, leaning hard into them, skidding, and coming close to hitting cars coming from the other direction.

I saw Mac's car swerve as he nearly hit the same cars. I heard horns and the screeching of brakes. I saw dust as he hit the shoulder. But after some fishtailing, he regained control and roared closer. He was a skillful driver, or very lucky, I'll give him that. I hoped he would lose control and go off on one of the curves but as I neared the first intersection he was gaining on me, fast. I had to take the chance on the switchback, or he would run over me.

I swung wide and leaned hard into the turn. I could sense the car close behind me... but could not look. I had to concentrate on navigating between a guard rail on the far side of the side road and an oncoming car. I skidded and wound up sliding down the shoulder on my backside in the reverse direction. I watched the scene unfold behind me as if it were in slow motion.

The car on the side road braked and skidded, narrowly avoided hitting Mac's car as he skidded past, and spun to a stop facing back down the side road. Mac sideswiped the guard rail, swerved across the road into the ditch, came out of the ditch, spun around a couple of times and came to a stop crossway in the road. I watched as Mac began to turn around. I was up and racing down the side road and trying to ignore the pain in my backside from sliding on the shoulder; the fear in me and the adrenaline was driving me.

I looked back and saw Mac coming on fast. In growing panic, I looked for a way out. Trees and bushes lined either side of the road. A construction yard was on the other side of the trees and bush on my left below the level of the road but there was no access on the side road. I came around a bend and saw a mound of gravel piled along the road making a break in the bushes.

I hoped it was solid enough as I cut left, hit the gravel and went airborne. I came down hard and cut hard to the right. The front tire caught a rut, flipped and threw me. I heard an awful crash behind me. All I could see was a cloud of dirt and gravel and I ducked and covered my head as rocks and dirt flew by me. The Pontiac landed, plowed through a pile of construction material and went over the embankment into the ditch along the turnpike below.

I did not wait to see if Mac was ok. The handle bars of my bike were crooked, the front wheel bent out of shape and the forks were bent. I picked up the bike and limped through the construction yard. I ducked behind a dump truck as people came running from the office and ran to the wrecked car. I hobbled to the exit onto Old York and carried my bike up the road to the airport less than a mile away. Police cars passed, heading toward the disturbance. I was glad they ignored me.

I was exhausted when I got to the flight school. Kelly was at an airshow near Philadelphia and Kim found me in a restroom washing my face. I had just been sick. "You look like you fight in a war." Kim said. "I saw your bike outside. You had an accident."

I described the fight and the chase.

"This fellow Mac is big trouble. I have heard of him. Maybe you need to stay away from him."

"Believe me I have never gone looking for him. His brother, John is in my high school class. I don't know if Mac knew who I was with this helmet. We have run into him and his brother before. I described the encounter in River Park the year before.

"You need to learn to defend yourself in case you run into him again." He asked. "Do you not know how to defend yourself, Michael?"

"I've fought off the occasional bully. My brother, Andy and I do some sparring."

"I do not mean fighting. I am talking about defending yourself. It is different."

"It is?"

"Yes, fighting means, he hits you and you hit back and get revenge. To defend means you avoid getting hit."

He made motions with his hands and as if he was deflecting a punch.

"You mean judo or ju-jitsu, or something like that. I don't know any of that. I'm not an athlete."

"It is not necessary to be an athlete."

"Yeah, but I'm not very big. I can't see someone like me throwing some big guy around."

"I am not bigger than you. Do you think I would be easy to beat?"

"Well no. You're older, smarter; and you were a soldier."

Kim shook his head, annoyed. "Ah! No need to be a soldier. Do not need to be big. Need to be smarter." He touched his head. "Smarter not to lose temper. Kim will teach you how to defend yourself if attacked again. Ok?"

"You can do that?"

"Yes, but you do not use what Kim teaches to take revenge. It is not for revenge. You must control temper. Learn to be patient. Let other fellow make his move. Use *his* move to defend yourself. That what means to be smarter."

He took me to his home which was a short distance from the airport. We took the bike to a Korean friend who had a bike shop. He offered to give me a used bike in exchange for my wrecked bike.

I met Kim's wife and children. We went to his garage, and he began illustrating judo and some blocking techniques. After that I practiced with Kim a couple of times a week after work.

But now I had to face Mom and Dad.

"Oh my God, McCaskey again." Mom was upset. "James, those… people are going to be the death of our children. I just know it."

"Mom…" I started to protest but stopped under her withering look.

My brother, Andy, said. "I don't know what you're gonna do. It will do no good to call the police. The township police are useless; they don't even patrol the roads. The chief deputy Krause hangs out at that bar in Etters…The Farm." He laughed and shook his head. "The only thing they grow there is trouble… fertilized by lots of booze." He laughed at his own joke.

"There may have been witnesses in KCs construction yard." I spoke. "Mac just missed hitting a car when I turned down Marsh Run. The police may have been called… there were lots of them on the road from New Cumberland. Mac wound up down over the embankment along the turnpike."

Dad said. "I will check to see if there was any report. You should have hung around and reported him to the police. The State Police will be involved if he was on turnpike property."

"I was too scared. I just wanted to get away from there."

"And you don't have the bike anymore for proof." Dad said.

CHAPTER 8

Early in the new school year the English literature teacher, Miss Wilson required us to prepare a report of our summer and present it before the class.

Miss Wilson chided me. "Michael, I wanted you to report on what you actually did, not one of your dreams. I want non-fiction not fiction. You *do* know the difference between fiction and non-fiction, do you not?" I was just describing flying with Mister Kelly.

I had expected some skepticism from the students, so I had brought pictures I got from Kim. He loved to take pictures. "This is true. It is not a dream." I showed pictures of Kim and me with Mister Kelly in the Stearman. "He took them after we got back." Fortunately, the mess on my pants did not show and I did not talk about that. I also showed pictures from the flight school. She let me continue until I talked about summer school.

"Things we have heard about other people who are different are often wrong. People attack others because they are different. The things we have been told about others are often lies based on prejudice and bigotry. Racism is not someone else's problem, like down south. It is right here, and it is our problem… everyone's. It affects us and our friends. Racism is another form of bullying. It is our responsibility to learn the truth and to stop…"

"That is enough, Michael." Miss Wilson interrupted me again. "I think we have heard enough about your summer. You may sit down now. We don't need to hear nonsense about racial discrimination. You are just repeating communist propaganda. That is un-American. Sit down."

"Yes, racism is un-American, and it is not communist prop…"

"Michael. *Sit down. Now.*"

Miss Wilson returned my paper with a failing grade. I asked about the grade, and she said that the subject was inappropriate and un-American, and I deserved a failing grade. I took the paper home and stashed it in a drawer. I did not show it to my parents though I had the feeling it was all wrong.

I talked to Chester Arnold, the advisor for rifle and the aviator's clubs, about joining the clubs. "You have not shown any interest in school clubs before this. Why now?"

I was reluctant to tell him I came because Connie and Eleanor Stevens had persuaded me and I shrugged and mumbled, "I don't know. I didn't think about it before this summer. Things changed." The girls were aspiring pilots. Connie's father was a naval officer at the naval base and Eleanor's father, an Army Air Force veteran, worked across the river at the air force base.

"You have a reputation for being a daydreamer, Michael. I can't have people daydreaming when they should be listening to safety instructions. Safety is important in shooting and flying. Lives depend on everyone paying attention. How can I be certain you will not just quit when you get bored with the lectures."

I mumbled. "America was built by dreamers. The pilgrims dreamed of a better life and the pioneers when they went west… not to mention the Wright Bros and Glen Curtiss."

"But they didn't just dream, they did something about it."

"Th… that is what I am trying to do. I qualified in CMP-NRA at Camp Perry this summer and I have earned a merit badge for shooting from the Boy Scouts and I have been going to ground school at the airport all summer."

Mister Arnold nodded. "Well ok. But I will be watching you… however; you are not old enough to get a student license for flying."

"Am I too old to join the club?"

"No, you are not too old for that."

"I turn sixteen in December. I can learn stuff until then… like I do at the airport."

I went with my dad to Collins garage in Etters when he went to get his car ready for winter. I roamed around the scrap yard out back while the work was being done. Mister Collin's Dobermans, Athena and Apollo followed me around sniffing my leg. I found an old truck and I poked around, climbing inside, sitting in the driver's seat… daydreaming about fixing it up. I wanted to have my own vehicle; I would also be old enough to get my driver's license in December.

Mister Collins found me sitting in the cab of the truck. "Michael, I wondered if the dogs had eaten you." He laughed.

"Yeah, they *are* interested in me, aren't they?" The Dobermans sat nearby eyeing me…hungrily I thought.

Cecil laughed, "Athena looks like she knows you. Maybe you've been here before. Maybe late at night." He gave me a suspicious look.

"Me? Oh, uh," I felt warm. "You mean the game the guys play… running the gauntlet?"

"Yeah, I know about that. I'm not dumb. The kids like to run through the yard and outrun the dogs." He smiled. "Fortunately, Athena and Apollo know most of the kids. They like the game and would not bite, though they will take a piece of clothing now and then. Strangers are not so lucky."

I shrugged, grinning sheepishly. "Yeah, a couple of guys dared me, and I lost a chunk from the seat of my pants. I think it was Athena. I am sure she remembers." I watched Athena who was staring at me with what I thought was an amused look; or maybe an eager look, daring me to make a sudden move. She licked her chops a couple of times. "She looks hungry. You did feed her this morning, didn't you?"

"You're safe." He laughed. "You have a hungry look yourself. I see you looking all over my truck."

I grinned. "I was dreaming again… of fixing that up, but I don't have a license yet; or the money to fix it up. It looks like it needs a little work. I'm good at dreaming… though I do know a little about engines… from Dietrich's."

"Oh, it's really not in that bad a shape. A little sanding and paint will do for the body. The engine needs some work, but I am sure it will run. It depends on how extreme you want to be. I can let you have it for fifty bucks."

"My friend, Dennis just got an old Chevy, and his dad is helping him put an engine in it. His father will pay for most everything. I have few funds, but most of it goes for flight school and I just want something that runs. My scooter gets me around, but it is no good on snow or ice."

"I heard you were working for Karl Dietrich over to York Landing. I need someone to do cleanup and small work around here. Do you think you can find the time? I could use the help. It would only be for a couple of nights a week and you can work on the truck here. I have a mechanic but he's only part time."

"I work at Dietrich's a couple of days a week, and I was doing work at some farms near home for the summer, but there is not much to do now… just a few hours occasionally. Can I start today?"

He laughed. "Yes, I can use the help right now. I need the store room straightened up. My wife and CC complain about not being able to find anything in there."

"I'll let dad know I'll be hanging around a while. Uh, how much can you pay me?"

"Well, I *am* giving you the truck." Cecil grinned. "How does seventy five cents an hour sound?"

"Yeah, that would be great!"

Now I had two sources of income, Collins and Dietrich, and there was the Saturday work at the airport, though I did not actually get paid for that. I did get the training and after I turned sixteen, I could apply for an apprenticeship. Then I would get paid for that work.

I began driver training as soon as I became sixteen late in December and I applied for my student pilot's license and started driving class at school.

"I think you have too much on your plate, young man." Mom complained shortly after I passed my driving test in early January and got my student pilot license. I *was* very busy.

"Driving, flying school, working on that truck? Something has to give. I think you should limit your flying."

Dad said. "School is more important."

"My school grades are good. I am passing algebra, surprisingly… not the highest grades but good. Flying involves calculations on fuel, speed, and flight planning and that has helped with math."

"Your English literature classes have gone way down. You barely passed." Dad said.

Mom had a puzzled expression. "English was one of your best subjects, Michael. What's happening?"

"I think Miss Wilson has it in for me."

"Why would she have it in for you?"

"I don't know. She had us write papers and talk about our summer and I talked about summer school, the boat, and going to the flight classes. She did not like what I said for some reason. She thought I was telling stories. And now she keeps giving me bad marks for book reports. She doesn't believe they are true, and I think she is racist."

"Michael, that's a terrible thing to say." Mom said.

"What reports?" Jim asked.

"We were supposed to write reports on non-fiction subjects. I did reports about the Honda Point disaster and the America's Cup races. They were in *Ships and the Seas* magazines. She claimed they were fiction; even after I showed her the magazine stories, she would not change the grades. I wrote a paper in November around thanksgiving on race relations in America and how Indians, Negros, and Chinese have been mistreated for the last couple of centuries. She gave me an 'F' for that. In that first talk, I got an E for talking about how my summer school experience changed my ideas about people who are different, like Negroes."

"Let me see those papers. Did she give them back to you?"

"Yeah. I have them in a drawer somewhere."

"Let me see them."

"What made you write about race relations, Michael?" Mom asked.

"Dad is on that committee, and you have those ladies from work all the time. They are all different and you all get along and have a lot of fun. I told you about Kathy helping me with algebra. Until I got to know her, I always thought that Negroes were not as intelligent as white people… I am not sure where I got that. I thought a lot about my own prejudices, and I didn't like what I saw."

"Where did you hear that nonsense?" Dad asked.

"I am not sure, but I think Dennis's dad is prejudiced. Spending time with Kathy and working at the garage, with Cecil, made me think about all that. I've been working with Mister Collins, and CC… Cecilia… she's also in my class… and her aunt. CC is really smart and so are the other girls, Kathy, Marcia Thomas and Pete Simons, kids in my class. I looked up history books and old newspapers at the library. Negroes are not the only people discriminated against. That is where I got the stuff I wrote about in November. We were supposed to write on current events and that is in the news every day."

"Well, you picked a touchy subject. We have problems in Harrisburg and York County and too many people want to ignore them and brush them under the carpet." Dad said.

"That's what Mister Collins says."

"Nevertheless, you probably should be careful." Mom cautioned.

"Other kids liked what I wrote, and they don't usually like stuff I do. Some said they could not understand why I got such bad marks."

Dad took my papers. I did not know what he intended to do with them until they started appearing in the local weekly. Some were published in a Harrisburg newspaper. I forgot that Dad wrote a column for the local weekly and he contributed articles to the city newspaper; he could be quite expressive with his writing.

Miss Wilson cornered me in the hallway. "Michael, I do *not* appreciate being called to the principal's office and being told to keep my personal views to myself or being *told* they are not appropriate for the class."

"What does that have to do with me?" I asked warily.

"You carried tales to Mommy and Daddy, and they complained about your grades."

"They wondered why my grades were so low. I showed them the papers you rejected because of my racial views."

"I *did not* reject them because of your racial views."

"That isn't what you told me when I asked. You called my opinions socialist hogwash. You even told me those people are not the same as us. You said the grammar, the composition and the punctuation were good. So, what else could it have been?

"Mom and Dad are active on race relations committees in the district and Dad writes for the newspapers. I guess the school board reads the newspapers." She was not amused.

However, Miss Wilson grudgingly changed her teaching and grading. She made it clear she did not like the principal or a member of the school board visiting her classroom regularly. She found ways to express her displeasure with me, but her severe looks did not translate into actions; my grades improved. However, I did not write any more reports on social issues that year; I had other matters on my mind.

Kelly came into the pilot's lounge, "Michael, are you ready?"

"Yeah, I've checked out the Vagabond a couple of times. It is fueled and ready."

"Ok. Let's go. Show me what you know."

I liked the Vagabond because the seating was side-by-side, I could see over the cowling, *and* it had a radio. I needed to work on my communications skills.

It was a bright sunny March morning with little wind and the takeoff was smooth. I set out on a cross-country flight that took us over southeast Pennsylvania to Pottsville.

We returned to Harrisburg an hour later. As we taxied to the parking area, Kelly said. "Stop here." He unbuckled his belt and got out. "Take it around a couple of times. I'll wait here." Without another word, he stepped out and walked away leaving me in the plane by myself.

My heart was pounding. It dawned on me, I'm on my own. He wants me to fly solo! My mind was blank. I could not think. I experienced a moment of panic. "Oh God, this is it. My solo. I'm about to solo, and I can't think." I sat trying to calm myself and remember what to do. Kelly stood at the edge of the parking area and when I looked at him, he shrugged and motioned with his hands toward the field.

I took a breath, checked for traffic, released the brake and then hesitated; I almost forgot! I called ground control to get clearance and taxied to the end of the runway. I did a final check and called the tower for clearance. I was nervous as I taxied onto the runway, advanced the throttle and took off.

After checking for traffic and getting clearance, I entered the traffic pattern downwind. So far so good. I reported each leg as I turned and when I cut the engine to idle and entered the base lag. Turning onto final, I found I was too high. I tried to lose altitude but picked up too much speed and called for a missed approach. I was cleared to go around. I was a bundle of nerves, and I flew away from the airport, to the north and circled for a few minutes while I calmed my nerves.

I called the tower, was cleared and entered the pattern again. The approach was perfect, and the landing was smooth; perfect! I accelerated to take off again. After the second landing I taxied to the tarmac. I was moaning under my breath, oh boy, I screwed up. That will end this flight.

Kelly was relaxing in a lawn chair with a cup of coffee; Kim was squatting at his side and shaking his head.

Kelly shook his head, raised two fingers over his head and drew two circles in the air. He wants me to do two more landings. I better not mess this up.

I received clearance for a touch and go and took off. My landings were perfect, at least in my mind and I was happy with myself. However, Kelly signaled me to do three more go-arounds. On my last approach, I was high again. I remembered something that Kelly taught me. I put the airplane into a slip, lost the altitude, straightened out and landed perfectly just past the threshold. I was right proud of myself… until I taxied to the parking area. Kelly was not in his chair. I saw him in front of the hangar. He waved me to taxi to the hangar.

My imagination began to work overtime; he looks angry, or is it my imagination? He didn't like me doing that slip. As I taxied to the front of the hangar, I saw Kelly talking to Mom and Dad; Andy, my brother, was with them. "Oh crap." I muttered. "Mom and Dad saw me mess up."

When I secured the plane and climbed out. Kelly was standing with his fists on his hips. "So young man, are you proud of yourself?"

I swallowed nervously, "I guess I messed that up, didn't I?"

"Were you trying to show off?"

I looked at Mom and Dad, uncomfortable. Dad was expressionless. Mom covered her mouth with a hand.

She was trying to stifle a laugh. Why is she laughing?

Mister Arnold and Connie with several other students rushed out from the Pilot's Lounge and surrounded me. Andy cut a swath out of the tail of my shirt and raised it over his head triumphantly.

"Nice flying Michael. I'm glad to see you've been paying attention." Kelly said. "That last landing was picture perfect. You are almost a pilot. Now the real work begins."

Connie said. "You know you have to buy the whole airport cokes, Michael." They were all laughing.

"Don't look so scared. You only have to buy all of us cokes." Andy said.

Mom embarrassed me with hugs and kisses. Dad, true to form, was miserly with his praise, but the big grin on his face betrayed him; he was proud. I was a pilot… almost. Dad paid for the Cokes.

CHAPTER 9

My success fed my confidence and that affected other activities. I excelled in shooting competitions, helping the school win interscholastic competitions. I took a greater interest in Boy Scout activities, and I even went camping in the winter with the troop… normally I disliked camping. The martial arts training had a lot to do with building my self-confidence.

On the other hand, I began to neglect church, to Mom's displeasure. As spring arrived, I preferred spending Sunday sailing, camping or working on the truck. Dad was on my side… or at least he did not discourage me, which also upset my mother.

I went to the airport to fly for a half-an-hour and work in the shop on Sunday afternoons. Since Kim went to church with his family on Sundays, I began to work with Doug Crombie in the electronics shop and took an interest in electronics.

My mother worried that I was becoming prideful. She stressed that I needed to seek after God and all those things would go better. But as far as I could see; as far as I wanted to see, I was fulfilling my dreams without God's help. To be honest, I felt that I did not need God. I was doing fine at everything without him or the church.

Dennis and I had been practicing, throwing and catching the baseball and he thought I was ready for my debut. I thought I was doing very well without making a public spectacle of myself; I still remembered the game last summer and I doubted that I could contribute to the team. However, Mister Lockhart, ever the optimist, and George Armstrong, the senior baseball coach, had other ideas. Lockhart caught up with me during gym period.

"You're kidding, aren't you? You've seen me play ball."

"Yes, I have, and you can be good with a little practice." He put an arm around my shoulders. "Dennis tells me you two have been practicing. You need to put that to some use… and we need more men on the bench."

"Oh, Dennis put you up to this." I laughed and glanced at my pal standing off to the side trying to look innocent. "A little practice huh?"

"Well, maybe a lot of practice." Lockhart grinned. "But I have confidence in you, and so does your pal."

"Yeah. My pal, Dennis." I looked at Dennis, pretending to be more annoyed than I was. He grinned and I just shook my head; we could *annoy* each other silly sometimes.

"Come out to practice. It cannot hurt to try." Lockhart urged.

"I don't know if I will have time for that. I work most evenings. Between Mister Dietrich and Mister Collins, flying every other weekend, and working at the airport, not to mention Boy Scouts. I think my plate is full as my mother and father would say, especially Mom."

He spoke. "We practice on Thursday during afternoon gym period and sometimes right after school. The games are on Fridays."

I shrugged and we left it at that. But my curiosity got the best of me and when Dietrich decided to change my hours, I found myself free on Thursdays after school; I decided to go to the practice. I had second thoughts when I saw John McCaskey there. He made his displeasure plain.

I became comfortable playing right field and did quite well. John played left field most of the year and we were on opposite sides of the field. I did not have to worry about being run down at home plate; since we were on the same team.

John tried to show off, throwing the ball all the way from the outfield to home plate. His pitches were far enough but they were *always* off target. Mister Armstrong was frustrated trying to get him to use the relay man.

Everything went well for several games, and I made the occasional spectacular play, making a diving catch or climbing the fence to catch a fly ball. Many balls got by me, but I was no worse than most of the other guys. I found I could hit the ball pretty good, and I learned to bunt. We won some games with a little help from me.

Ironically, John, who fancied himself a good player, made more errors than anyone, and several of our losses could be laid at his feet. He was *not* a team player.

Dennis and I took part in boating events at the annual Spring Fair in York Landing. Dennis crewed with me for sailing races, and I helped him when he raced his runabout in the power boat events. We helped the race marshals with some events with the younger kids. With all the boats on the river, the marshals were kept busy keeping boaters a safe distance from the sailboats. Most of the people partied and watched from pontoon boats.

The younger kids were racing Optimist sailboats and they completed one leg of the course when a few boats overturned. Rescue boats pulled children from the water and recovered overturned boats while the remaining boats continued the race. The kids were nearing the final marker and preparing to turn for home when a speed boat raced in from upriver right through the middle of the flotilla of small sailboats. The young sailors panicked; boats collided and overturned and became entangled. A girl became trapped under a sail and by the time she was pulled out she was unconscious. She was rushed to shore while Marshals and deputies boarded boats and raced out to the scene. Dennis and I were helping other crews rescue kids when a woman yelled. "Hey! Those idiots are coming back."

I looked upriver and saw the hooligans' boat speeding toward us.

"Oh crap." Dennis said. "That's that idiot, McCaskey."

"What's he doing?" I spoke.

John was standing at the gunwale of the boat, a paddle raised like a baseball bat. The boat was coming right at us. Dennis said. "Is he coming after us? I think he's coming after us."

"It looks like it." I looked around for something to defend myself with and as I considered an oar, my eye fell on the flare gun. It was kept loaded and ready to signal for help. I fired the flare at the approaching boat. The driver ducked and turned abruptly and although the flare did not come close to him, it just missed John. He ducked and the sudden movement of the boat threw him off balance and he went over the side into the water.

The flare landed in the back of the boat and sparked panic. Two of the boys leaped overboard as the driver rushed to put the fire out. He tossed the flaming gas tank overboard, extinguished the flames in the boat and somehow picked up the flare and tossed it off the boat. The gas tank exploded with a muffled bang and the whoosh of a fountain of water. Race marshals and police arrived and seized the boat and its soaked crew.

All of the children were rescued and although the race was doomed the girl was revived and rushed to the hospital. We all learned later that she was recovering ok and was more concerned that she did not finish the race.

The rest of the weekend went well. Dennis won his power boat race handily and I finished second in a close sailboat race, leading for the last leg until the last second.

John came to school the following week. Several of us were wondering why he was not in jail. John glared at me all week, breathing threats and making nasty comments. I ignored him hoping he would tire of the nonsense.

I had a feeling that we were headed for trouble when John came to practice on Thursday. He growled at me. "You Son-of-a-bitch. You could have killed one of us with that flare. The gas tank was on fire."

"You almost killed a little girl. I don't know why the judge let you off."

"You people were hogging the river. Sailboats have no business on the river."

"The river is big enough for everyone and everyone was enjoying the day until you guys came along."

Armstrong interrupted his rant and made us get busy with the practice. Lockhart kept us apart, for the moment.

Lockhart said the justice-of-the-peace released John and two of the others because they were juveniles. They were fined for mischief. The boat operator was charged but was out on bail.

John came out to play ball on Friday; still uttering threats.

Everything was ok until the eighth inning. Carl was injured when John ran into him, ignoring Carl's call for the ball. John was moved to centerfield for the top of the ninth inning. We were leading by two runs. The first batter hit a ground ball to me, and I threw to second to hold the runner at first. John was preoccupied ridiculing my weak arm when the second batter hit a fly ball to center. I ran to back up John expecting him to catch an easy fly ball. He caught many fly balls and it appeared to me that he would make an easy catch, but the ball bounced off his glove. I caught it on the fly before it hit the ground putting the batter out. The runner on first tagged up and tried to make it to second. I tried to throw to second to stop him; it would be close; he had a good jump. As I threw the ball John reached out yelling. "That's my ball!"

When I threw the ball, John stuck his glove out and knocked it down. He rushed to pick it up and threw it to third as the runner raced toward third. However, his throw was off target, as usual, and went to the fence. The runner raced home before the ball could be retrieved.

John came after me. "You made me miss it."

"I was backing you up like I'm supposed to. That's why they call it a *team*. You should be watching the ball instead of me. You screwed up, John. You always screw up because you like to grandstand. You are not a team player."

"You distracted me and made me miss."

I was tiring of his nonsense. "You should have thrown the ball to the short stop. He could have gotten the runner at third."

I scrambled away as he made as if to club me. Armstrong's yell stopped him, but he continued to utter threats as the next batter came up. The batter hit a single to center field.

The next batter hit the ball down the right field line, and I raced for it, dove and caught it in the webbing of my glove. I landed hard on my stomach, but I came up throwing and stopped the runner at second.

The other team seemed to be cueing on our trouble in right field because the next batter hit a high fly to right field. I called for it as I ran in, and John knocked me down as I was about to catch it. The ball bounced past us and headed for the fence. I ran the ball down at the fence and threw it to Dennis at first base. The runner took off from second base, had rounded third and was eating up the base path intent on making it home on our error.

I did not see whether Dennis got him at home as John knocked me down again. I rolled away to avoid a vicious kick, jumped up and ran to the side line to keep away from the brute. He took another swipe at me.

He yelled. "I am going to teach you to stay out of my way, moron."

"It was my ball, stop acting like a baby. No on second thought babies behave better."

He growled... *he actually growled*, and I ducked again as he bolted after me.

I heard cheering from the crowd and glanced quickly to see that Dennis had gotten the runner at home. But I became distracted, frantic, trying to escape as I ran toward the infield. John followed me, swung and knocked my hat off.

"What's your problem? Knock it off. The game's over. We won... no thanks to you." I yelled.

"I don't care. I'm going to pound you."

"Yeah, it's always about you isn't it. It's a team sport jerk... you need to play for the team and not for yourself." He knocked me on the head with his glove. "Hey stop that. There's no need for you to be hitting me."

"I'll do more than hit you, Hunter. I owe you. You've been a pain in my ass for a long time and I aim to correct that."

"What are you talking about I've never done anything to you." I retrieved my hat, but he knocked it off again. I yelled at the first base umpire. "Aren't you going to do anything, Ump?"

"If you can't stand the heat, boy, get out of the kitchen."

I stared at him. And then as I leaned down to pick up my hat John stepped up to try and hit me again. I brought my glove up in a backhand motion and caught him in the groin. He stopped, bending over, grabbing his midsection. His face was right there and too much of a temptation. I put my weight into the swing as I focused on his chin. I felt the pain shoot through my fist and up my arm as I stumbled back off balance. I was nursing my hand and wrist and setting myself for John's retaliation. But John just stood there, a puzzled look on his face and then fell face first onto the turf. I stared at him, surprised at the ease of knocking him down. He seemed to be out cold or dazed; he moaned and tried to push up. He rolled over and laid spread-eagle on the grass.

I heard the crowd noise suddenly go quiet and then begin to rise again. I glanced at the people lining the fence to see a lot of thumbs up, clapping, cheering and laughing… apparently at John's expense.

I looked at the ump and spoke. "I put the fire out."

I retrieved my hat and turned to walk back to the bench and found myself surrounded by the team. Lockhart draped his arm around my shoulder.

"I guess that arm is stronger than we thought." He glanced back at John still laying spread eagle on the ground.

John did, eventually, stagger off the field but was still out of it as we all left the field savoring a rare victory, one of the few we would enjoy that spring.

John came after me, again, in the hallway on Monday, seeking revenge. John kept pushing and Coach Cord and Principal Martin, apparently tired of John's trouble making, intervened. Cord ordered us to settle our differences in the ring. Martin agreed but I was not so sure about that.

I was not adept at boxing, though I sparred occasionally with my brother. Kim's training did not include boxing lessons although it did include blocking moves. At barely 120 pounds, I was a light weight and no match for John; he outweighed me by 70 or 80 pounds.

However, it turned out that John was no boxer either and the fight went on for several minutes. His weight and bulk worked against him. I landed blows to his face, blocking and sidestepping his clumsy jabs and wild swings. Blows to his face seemed to have little effect. I could not get a solid hit on his apparently glass jaw. He staggered me with the occasional hit and knocked me down twice with blows to my shoulder or chest. Cord stopped him from kicking me while I was down which only seemed to anger him more. He seemed to want to stomp on me in spite of Cord's angry rebukes. I got up and tried to avoid close contact, making him pursue me around the mats. We were both tiring, and he was getting frustrated. I probed his defenses, getting in some solid upper cuts as he held his gloves high to protect his face. I landed a couple of hard hits to his midriff, and he dropped his gloves to protect his midsection. He apparently thought I was going to hit him in the groin again. I saw an opening and pounded his face hard with several blows, staggering him. He dropped his guard as he staggered back and I followed up, hitting him repeatedly. It was becoming easier to avoid his weak and clumsy swings.

The students cheered as he went down after stumbling on the edge of the mat. He got up and charged at me trying to grapple. I used judo to throw him over my hip onto the mat. He kept coming at me until I threw him down again. Frustrated, he tore off the gloves and charged at me.

Coach Cord tried to intervene, and John punched him in the face. Cord fell on the hard wood floor off the mats, stunned, his face bloodied. Some students, football players, tried to stop John but he turned on them, punching and kicking. He threw them aside easily and came after me.

I was trying to shed my gloves when John pinned me against the wall and began choking me. I tried to use martial arts blows to break his hold, to no avail; we were too close together. John was out of control, and I began to panic. He was too strong for me. I was on the verge of blacking out when I drove my knee into his groin twice. He backed away, loosening his grip. I stumbled away from the wall, making space to move. I tried to catch my breath as he came at me again. I unleashed a series of rapid karate kicks to his stomach and chest, knocking him backward and off the mats. I landed a strong reverse kick to his face, hitting him right on the jaw. He fell on the hard floor spitting blood. I was breathing hard, and my neck was sore, but I worried for a moment that I had kicked him too hard. He was breathing but he did not try to get up. Someone said he was crying, but I did not see that. Miss Ketterman, the school nurse, checked him and said he had a broken jaw. She had him sent to the hospital.

John was expelled from school for striking Coach Cord. Several boys were nursing bruises, black eyes and fat lips. Fortunately, football season was long past, and they had plenty of time to recover before next year.

Many students were not shy about their relief that John was gone. Teachers and staff were less open but there was a palpable sense of relief in many classes. John had bullied girls, boys and even intimidated some teachers, especially women.

I reveled in my new-found popularity, a change from the past when I felt like an outsider and scorned.

My mother worried all the more that my success was going to my head, even though she was relieved that John had gotten his due. I had the feeling Dad was beginning to worry about my attitude. He did not say anything… but that was the rub… he didn't say *anything*. I thought my triumph should be cause for celebration, not remorse.

CHAPTER 10

Dad took his old Desoto to be repainted at Carlisle's body shop in the spring. My truck was finally ready to be painted and Mister Carlisle offered to do both vehicles, for a reasonable price, since he would have to mix a large batch of paint anyway and he could use the left over on my truck. The old truck had a wooden box that dad helped me build and only the relatively small cab would need painting.

I picked up the freshly painted truck a week later and went to Collins garage. Cecilia had ridden her bike to the store to pick up small parts. She called to say a heavy part had come in and she could not carry it. Mister Collins asked me to go pick her up.

I arrived at the auto store to see Cecilia surrounded by a gang of thugs. Mac was leaning against his car, the infamous Pontiac… watching his pals hassle her. The car showed quite a few battle scars from our earlier encounter. It had a crumpled fender, a crooked bumper and the hood was held on by a rope. People were watching from across the street at a restaurant, a hairdresser, and other stores but no one tried to intervene.

I parked and approached the gang of thugs. My stomach was in a knot as I thought about taking on five guys. My new found confidence had not deluded me into thinking I was invincible. But seeing the thugs surrounding Cecilia angered me and though I was aware of the many warnings about losing my temper, I really wanted to hammer these thugs.

She was backed up against the railing over the truck pit and had nowhere to go. A thug grabbed the hem of her skirt and tried to lift it as they laughed and made crude racist remarks.

I yelled, *"Hey, get away from her."*

The fellow let go of her skirt and turned but I was on top of him and chopped him in the neck with my elbow. I was pleased to see him drop like a sack of potatoes. The second fellow came at me, and I lifted my foot and planted a kick on his solar plexus that sent him down the driveway and into the truck dock.

I turned to confront Mac and the other two guys. "You bunch of cowards are big and tough when picking on old people and girls. You need to get in that pile of junk and leave… now! You're done here."

"Do you know who I am boy?"

"Do I *know* you? Yeah, I know you. You think you're special, but you are just a coward and a thug. You pick on people you think are too weak to fight back."

Mac laughed. "And *you* think you can beat me?" He took in my short slim physique and laughed again. He gestured at the two thugs on the ground. "You caught them by surprise. Do you think I will be *that* easy?"

Cecilia quietly said. "Michael, be careful."

"I've fought with you before." I scoffed "*Mac the Hammer.* Big deal. I broke your arm on River Road two years ago." He perked up showing signs of interest. "You and your cronies ran off like whipped dogs. Your brother squealed like a stuck pig." I goaded him knowing I was asking for trouble, and I got carried away with my antagonism. In retrospect my beating of John may have been going to my head. I really *wanted* to pound these guys. Mac's eyes opened and his look darkened. "I have beaten this fat boy here a couple of times in seventh and eighth grade." I jerked my head toward one of his cronies.

Cecilia sounded shocked. *"Michael!"*

I laughed. "You chased me down Marsh Run last summer." I glanced at the Pontiac parked near the road. "I am surprised you got that piece of junk running again."

He was standing up now, like a snake coiled to strike, but I pushed on, my heart beating with anticipation… or maybe fear. It was a little of both, something I would experience often later in situations where I knew I could be hurt… or killed. The adrenalin was pumping.

I prodded a little more. "I kicked the crap out of your *little* brother a month ago." My heart was pounding, expecting his attack. It was obvious he was becoming angry, but he still seemed uncertain. I thought I actually had him intimidated. "I hear you like to beat down guys you think insulted your mother. *You* are an even bigger insult to your mother, the way you strut around bullying everyone. I'm sure she is proud of you."

He launched himself at me and I blocked the punch, seized his wrist and tossed him over my hip. He flipped head over heels onto the ground, struck his head on the railing guarding the truck pit, rolled under the rail and fell four feet to the bottom of the pit. He landed awkwardly and let out a pained shriek.

I met fat boy's attack with a reverse kick to his chest stopping him in his tracks. I saw the last man approaching out of the corner of my eye and dropped down. A chain passed over my head and I swept out with my leg, taking his legs from under him. He went down and I was up and facing fat boy again as he came back. I landed several kicks finishing with a hard blow to his solar plexus. He pitched backward and rolled down the driveway.

I heard Cecilia's warning. The fellow with the chain was up and coming on again. I just had time to leap over the chain as he tried to take my feet out from under me. As I leaped, I twisted and lashed out with a foot and caught him in the face. I landed on both feet, spun and sent him flying backward with a kick to his chest. He bounced off the side of the car and collapsed moaning on the drive.

I turned to see fat boy high-tailing it up the road. I turned to face the first two thugs as they were finally getting to their feet. However, they rushed to help their boss as he half crawled and limped out of the truck pit. Mac appeared to have an injured leg. He needed his friends to help him get to his car. He stopped and glared at me. "You haven't seen the last of me boy. I will be back to finish this. You're a dead man." They piled into the Pontiac and sped off.

"You and what army?"

Cecilia stood against the wall of the shop, a frightened look on her face. "Are you all right CC?" I asked.

"I–I don't know, Michael, am I?" She stared at me, a frightened look on her face.

I was puzzled and it occurred to me, she's scared of me. "Come on, CC. you know me. You don't have to be scared of me."

"I am not sure I know you. I–I mean I *am* grateful for your help." She looked across the road. "No one else would." The people across the road were disappearing quickly. "But I don't know. I–I've never seen you like this."

"What don't you know?"

"You've changed. You were always so nice and happy, so quiet and nice to be around… but now you are… you are so bold… aggressive. Even… uh, arrogant." She looked uncomfortable.

I was still keyed up from the fray and was not too careful of my answer. "Yes. I *have* changed. I don't understand why it is all that bad. I like to think of it as confident. Maybe I am not the shy fearful little boy of seventh grade. I have learned to take care of myself." I answered smugly and thought, she sounded like my mother. I tried to change the subject. "If we are finished here maybe we can get back to the shop."

I loaded her bike, and put the heavy part into the truck, and we drove back to the shop in silence. I brooded at her criticism… I guess I thought she *should* be more grateful.

"Michael."

"What?" I snapped, still nursing my feelings.

"I'm sorry. I am not sounding very grateful. You helped me and I sound so ungrateful. Thank you for rescuing me."

I smiled finally. "You're my friend, CC. I will always help you."

"Thank you. You *are* a friend." She seemed to relax and kissed me on the cheek. I felt warm all over as the tension released. She laughed. "You are my white knight."

I laughed at that. "We better not let your uncle see us. He might think we are making out; then I might be your banished knight." She blushed and giggled.

The story of the fight made the rounds in the township. At first, I stayed anonymous since I was not that well known. Stories told of a *hero* in the fedora and driving a black pickup truck. Then I could not go anywhere without having people whisper and point. It was fun for a while but then my natural reserve kicked in and I wanted to hide. I changed to wearing a ball cap for a while and riding the scooter around; it was late spring, and summer and most days were sunny.

One day a customer at the garage cornered me. "Hey, ain't you the kid that whipped the McCaskey gang?"

I looked around pretending confusion. "Me? Gosh Mister, do I look like I could beat up a whole gang of thugs?" I laughed. "Don't I wish? I am so notorious for clumsiness at school I am the last kid they pick for games in gym period."

Mister Collins leaned close and whispered. "I think the lad protests too much." I got quiet. I got amused looks from Cecilia.

The fellow scratched his head. "Yeah, you don't *look* like you could fight. But I see you drive a black pickup."

Mister Collins interrupted. "John, there are many black pickups in the county, I know because I service them. *Your* car is ready."

However, although I became uncomfortable when people brought it up, I was proud of myself and took it all in.

Dad was pleased and Mom was proud of me standing up for Cecilia, but she still worried that I was becoming too prideful. She counselled that it was going to lead to trouble. "Pride goes before the fall." She would say. But I dismissed that. I did not think I was being proud and did not want to hear that. I told her she was beginning to sound like a stuck record. She looked disappointed and I felt unkind.

CHAPTER 11

Over the summer my flying hours built up and I began to venture farther and farther afield practicing navigation. I planned my first cross country flight with Carl Anderson, an older instructor. We were to fly to Allentown and Lancaster and then return to Harrisburg.

It was a clear morning with little wind when we took off and headed east. The first leg went smoothly except Mister Andersen complained of indigestion all the way. From the time we took off he consumed antacids like candy, and I suggested he should see a doctor. He became angry and told me to mind my own business. He pointed out I had enough to do flying the airplane without trying to play doctor.

We took a short break at Allentown and then we took off on the second leg to Lancaster. Thirteen minutes out of Allentown, Andersen doubled over with pain and became pale. I became worried. He was unsteady and incoherent. I asked him a question, but he did not answer. I looked carefully and saw that he was passed out and leaning against the window. There was blood at the corner of his mouth. I nearly panicked.

I got my thoughts together and declared a medical emergency. I received clearance to fly straight in to the Reading Airport three minutes away. The landing went smoothly, and an ambulance met us. Andersen was vomiting blood as he was rushed to the hospital.

I learned that he had a bleeding ulcer. I called Kelly at Harrisburg, and he told me that Anderson had been seeing a doctor about stomach problems. Kelly said he would send someone out, but I said that I could fly the plane back to Harrisburg ok and he approved, though he did sound reluctant. I skipped the Lancaster leg and flew directly back to the Harrisburg Airport.

I began instrument training late in the summer and Kelly went with me on a supervised IFR flight from Harrisburg to Wilkes-Barre-Scranton and back over the Blue Ridge Mountains. Other pilots saw that it was unusual for Kelly to take students over the mountains because of the notorious mists that made flying difficult for inexperienced pilots.

As expected, we met the Appalachian mists, and I experienced the effects of disorientation which caused pilots to lose control over the mountains. Fortunately, Kelly was there to keep me out of trouble, and we completed the flight with no problems.

"Michael, we'd like to talk with you." Connie Sat next to me in the library. The senior year had barely started, and I was hitting the books, studying in the library, a change from my daydreaming days. She got my full attention but then I saw she was not alone. I was surrounded by a gang of girls. I wondered what was up as my heart beat increased. Kathy, CC, and others sat down around the table. I imagined I looked like a deer in the headlights with all those lovely girls surrounding me. I had mixed feelings, being surrounded by a covey of pretty girls. For all my new-found self-confidence, I was still intimidated by girls.

"Oh, don't look so scared, Michael. We don't bite. We just want to talk." Connie said.

"Uh-huh. What about?" I might have enjoyed the situation, but my sense of danger was aroused.

"We are concerned." Eleanor Stevens moved up close on my other side. Eleanor had long lush tresses and a cute pixie like face. Dimples marked her smooth cheeks when she smiled, which was often. She did not help calm my pulse. "You have not been involved in many class events. We feel you are missing out on so much of high school."

"*Ahem.* I am in the rifle club and the aviator's club. I think I am very involved. Oh, and I played baseball last year… don't forget that."

"Oh yes. How could we? And that's all the more reason we wanted to talk to you." Connie said.

"You seldom attend socials or dances… or football games." Carol said. "We feel you need to come out and support the team, even if you don't play."

"Whoa you are *not* going to get me out on that field. No way." I threw my hands up in defense. "I have never had any interest in football, and I cannot dance worth a darn."

"Oh relax. We don't need you to play football just come and cheer… and dance."

"I can't dance."

CC countered, laying a hand on my shoulder. "Michael, I've seen your *moves*. You have no excuse." I looked at her and she reacted with pursed lips and raised eyebrows, daring me to say something. "I'm talking about dancing."

There was a chorus of *yesses!* And Connie said, "Yeah, hat man, we have heard of your skills... as dubious as they may be. They need to be applied to more constructive pursuits."

"I have not always felt welcome at school affairs." I looked around lamely. "Present company accepted, of course."

"We get caught up in our own affairs and don't always think about other kids. But we want to make up for that." Eleanor lamented.

"You know how I am with sports. I'm really not that interested."

Carol leaned across the table and smiled. "You say that, but we've seen you play. I saw you chase down Terry and tackle him once... in ninth grade... and then there *was* the aforementioned baseball last year."

"Yes." Connie added. "And I remember Gifford's Point. You were a lot better than John in that game." There was a chorus of agreement. "I think you may have gotten even with him on that score... last year."

"Better than John." I scoffed. "That's not saying much. The cheerleaders would be better than John, and tackling Terry almost killed me."

"Michael, we are not asking you to play. We would like you to come out and cheer for the team... and come to the dances... please." Connie pleaded, holding my arm and batting her eyes.

"Michael, you can't blame it all on everyone else." Wanda, a tall beautiful blonde from Scandinavia, joined the gang-up. "You always keep to yourself. You should not be so bashful. I know that's no excuse for people being mean but..."

"Bashful?" Kathy spoke up. "He wasn't so bashful in summer school."

"When you kissed me two years ago at Gifford's Park you weren't..." Connie started but was interrupted by Kathy.

"What? Wait. He kissed *you* at Gifford's Park? Two years ago?" Kathy pretended shock. "I wasn't your first? *Michael!*" Kathy scowled impishly, her fists on her hips.

I was turning my head looking from one to the other so fast, I thought I should have whiplash.

Connie, in mock horror, protested, "How many girls have you been...?"

"Wait. Wait. Girls now let's not get carried away..."

Wanda chortled. "Georgie Porgie, puddin' and pie, kissed the girls and made them cry, when the boys came out to play, Georgie Porgie ran away." The girls were laughing at my discomfort.

Eleanor cleared her throat. "I think I was his first."

"What?" A chorus of voices filled the library to Miss Rose's displeasure as she scowled in our direction and shushed us.

"He kissed me... or tried to, at Boomer's birthday party. It wasn't much of a kiss. I thought a fly landed on my cheek. He thought I was his aunt. I hope you all had better results."

"Ok. Ok ladies. I'll go to your football game. Let's just forget all this."

"Forget? Forget that you've been fooling around behind my... *our* backs." Connie stood with her fists on her hips, an unconvincing scowl on her face. There was a round of laughter at my expense. Miss Rose was not amused.

"Now just wait one minute… *ladies!*" I weakly protested. "I seem to remember you had a ring around your neck, and *you.*" I turned to Kathy, "*You* were making plans to ambush Pete." Her mouth opened in shock, but I turned to Eleanor. "I will be happy to make up for that." I smiled and gave her an eager look. "I am sure I can do better. You know what they say; practice makes perfect." I grinned mischievously. "Soon?"

She played with a strand of hair and bit her lip coyly.

"Ok ladies." Carol protested. "I think we are getting *waaayy* off the subject here. Michael. *You* have no more excuses." She raised her eyebrows. "You *have* to come to the game tonight and that is final. We will come to your house and get you if you are not there." She thumped her finger on my shoulder. "Or maybe we'll spread rumors in the locker room… about you kissing all the girls."

"Yes, maybe we should check with Audrey. She asked him to the Sadie Hawkins Day dance last year. How did that work out, Don Juan?" Bonnie Harris said. There followed a chorus of agreement.

I found it impossible to resist the onslaught. I was wallowing in the attention in spite of the feeling of embarrassment. "Just remember. I warned you I can't dance."

"That is no excuse. Most of *you* guys can't dance and we have to dance with each other."

"Monty is pretty good." Someone said.

"We can't *all* dance with Monty." Someone murmured.

I began to attend the football games and found them enjoyable. I even made it to the dances after the games and I did learn to dance a little better. However, I irritated Miss Wilson again because she saw me dancing with the black girls. But when she mentioned it, I pointed out that all of the guys were dancing with the black girls, "And why not?" I challenged, "They are part of the class like everyone else, and besides they are good dancers." She scowled but kept her peace and stood in a corner glaring angrily at all the rebellious teenagers. I liked to think maybe I had something to do with that, though in truth our class was more open-minded than previous years. Miss Wilson brooded and fumed in the shadows along with the teacher's pets that seemed glued to her side.

In October, I planned a solo cross country flight in a J-3 Piper Cub. I would have no instructor with me; a true solo flight. My destination was Ocean City, Maryland. It was two hours away on the Atlantic shore. On the return flight, I planned to stop at Bradley's field in Maryland to refuel. Bradley's was where Kelly practiced aerobatics.

I arrived in Ocean City on time with no problems and I was feeling proud of myself. With the tail wind I made it in just two hours and used just over half of my fuel. I got my log book signed and then left for Bradley's field, on the East shore of Chesapeake Bay.

On that flight I met a head wind, and I was consuming more fuel than I expected. I regretted not refueling at Ocean City. But I was sure I had enough to make it to Bradley's. I began to have second thoughts.

And I thought if Kelly was there doing aerobatics, he would not appreciate me flying into the area with no warning.

Crap, I knew I messed up. This was a big mistake… I was not feeling so proud all of a sudden. I was making too many mistakes. I needed to change my destination. I was minutes from Bradley's when I calculated my fuel and found it was much lower than I had thought. I checked the map for a nearby field where I could top up. I had few options. Winslow's Field, a private airfield, was in my line of flight and I landed there.

A note on the office door announced the airfield was closed due to the death of Mister Winslow. There was no one around and it was getting cold. I'd freeze my butt off if I tried to sleep in the plane. There were no towns nearby. I thought of breaking into the office and getting the keys to unlock the pump. I was undecided and it would be getting dark soon. With no electrical system the J-3 had no lights, and I couldn't fly after sunset.

I needed to do something. I got out the charts. Everything upwind was out of the question. I looked at the gas gauge… the rod was just peeking above the gas cap in front of the windscreen with less than an inch of red showing, the hook on the end hovering above the cap. I made a rough estimate that I had about 20 minutes of fuel. There was another airfield a few miles south about five minutes away.

I had another dilemma; the J-3 needs someone to turn the prop to start it. I found a block for the wheel, set the magnetos to off, fuel to off, and turned the prop three times and set it at the top of the compression cycle. I had never done this before, and I kept imagining getting my head cut off. I set the magnetos to 'both' and cracked the throttle. I pulled the prop through and jumped back to keep from being hit by the spinning prop. It sputtered and died. I was nervous as I repeated the procedure; magneto off, throttle closed, crank the prop twice and set… magnetos on, crack the throttle. I opened the throttle a little more this time. I pulled the prop through, expecting to get hit by the spinning prop. I could envision me lying on the ground with my arms chopped off. However, it started this time and ran a little fast. I rushed around the wing tip avoiding the prop and pulled the throttle back a little to slow the racing engine but not so much as to turn it off. I should have pulled it back further because when I removed the block from the wheel the airplane began to move, with me standing outside. Fortunately, I was able to hold it back long enough for me to climb in and get my feet on the brakes and pull the throttle back to slow the engine further. I breathed a sigh of relief, visualizing the plane, with me hanging out, crashing into the woods on the other side of the strip. I rested to get my breath and fasten the seat belt before taking off.

I landed at Freetown airfield to find it had no fuel facilities and it was too late for me to try for another field; the sun was setting. The residents of a nearby farm offered me a bed for the night.

Mrs. Robertson woke me early and fed me a breakfast of eggs and bacon. Mr. and Mrs. Robertson were very hospitable and helpful. There was no fuel at the field, but Mr. Robertson said that some locals used white gas from a local gas station; regular auto gas did not work well in plane engines. He supplied a five gallon can. After I poured the fuel into the tank, Mr. Robinson was reluctant to prop the plane. It is a dangerous job. Mrs. Robinson worried when I decided to prop it myself. I went through the same procedure as before. To my pleasant surprise, the airplane started on the first try and ran as smoothly as you please. Practice makes perfect, they say. I was getting cocky again.

At Robinson's suggestion I flew to Bay Bridge Airport twenty miles to the southwest. My only concern was that the flight took me out over the bay past Rush Island. I worried for all of the four minutes it took me to cross to Love Point. I arrived safely at Bay Bridge airfield, refueled, found someone to sign my log and someone to prop the plane. I made it back to Harrisburg with no further problems.

When I told Kelly about the flight he hit the ceiling. "You idiot! I go to Bradley's for a reason, to get away from traffic. The area was closed to traffic, which you would have known if you had checked your notices to pilots. You are getting too big for you britches young man. I will *not* sign your log for this. You made too many mistakes in your planning. There will be no more flying for you until next year."

"No!"

"No? What do you mean *no*, young man? I…"

"I mean no, sir. I *did* check the notices. There was no warning."

Kelly stared open mouthed. "Well…" he sputtered, "Yes… I mean, uh, no, there weren't because I was not there this weekend, but…" He looked flummoxed.

"And when I found that I was running low on fuel, I changed my flight plan… just like I would during a flight test. I did not make a mistake, Mister Kelly… I mean, uh, yes, I did make one mistake. I should have refueled at Ocean City, but I changed my plan and found an alternative, twice. And when it was obvious I could not make it to…"

"Ok. Ok. You didn't make *that* many mistakes. But–but." He wavered. "Ah crap, give me your log book." He signed it as I grinned. He gave me a scowl and muttered. "You're getting too big for your britches, young man."

Mom and Dad were not amused by my adventure. They scolded me for being impetuous. Mom was unwavering. "*You* are heading for a fall young man, and you better straighten up."

CHAPTER 12

The last football game of the season was at York just before Thanksgiving. York was our arch rival and they were unbeaten. We were the worst team in the conference. They were on the verge of a championship. York was over-confident, made too many mistakes and it snowballed. What our team lacked in skill they made up for in enthusiasm, and Valleyview's clumsy team shut down the York offense. The guys took advantage of errors… several turnovers, and made the most of it, winning 14-3.

I went to the restroom right after the final whistle and when I came out, I walked into a riot. I barely avoided getting into it with the mob and I took refuge near the stands. Fights broke out, I assumed, because the York youths were frustrated at having their perfect season ruined by a wretched team such as ours. However, it soon became clear that outside forces were at work. Gangs of youths, who appeared to be older than high schoolers, roamed the field targeting anyone in the wrong school colors. Panicked families rushed their children to cars and buses.

I was too far from the main gate, and I tried to avoid roving gangs by hiding under the visitors' bleachers and working my way toward a maintenance gate at the back of the field. The gate was fairly close to where I parked my truck. As I skulked behind the bleachers, I saw Connie hiding and looking frightened. I joined her in the shadows of the stands, and we watched the mobs chasing hapless victims and wrecking the grandstand; the goal posts were being torn down.

Connie said, "I went to the restroom to change from my uniform and when I came out a gang came after me, but they became distracted when other people came out of the locker room wearing school jackets. I think they got away though. They ran for the main gate, but I was cut off." She pointed toward the main gate. "Look, the band and the football team are trying to run interference." She looked around warily. "How are *we* going to get out of here, Michael? There is a mob between us and the gate."

"We could stay here and wait for the police to restore order…"

"No. That gang is coming this way and looking under the bleachers." She pointed to several thugs with clubs and bats working their way along the stand and peering under the seats.

"We can make a run for that maintenance gate." I looked toward the parking area that was quickly being emptied. "It is right back here, and it is open… I saw people go out through it. It doesn't look like anyone is watching it now."

"Let's run for it. They'll find us if we stay here."

When we ran from the shelter of the bleachers, the gang saw us. I grabbed a discarded flag staff. "I'll see if I can hold these guys off. My truck is on the other side of this field."

I poked one thug in the gut and knocked a second down, clubbing him over the head. I took the legs from under the third and the last fellow ran off yelling for help.

I ran after Connie. "Those guys will be back when they get help. Let's go this way." We circled the field keeping to the shadows. The other side of the field was lit by cars rushing for the exit road. We circled the field until we were near the truck. Connie jumped in and slid across while I fumbled with the key. I got the truck started and we took a short cut across the field to a side road as the gang pelted us with rocks. We bounced crossed a shallow ditch, over the sidewalk, and out onto the road.

We stopped for a breather at a restaurant and took our time over coffee and a snack. Now that we were clear of the mobs and were able to quiet our nerves we laughed at the incident and celebrated our team's unexpected victory. We wondered if the police would be at the school, so we took our time, talking over our plans for the upcoming Thanksgiving week.

We arrived at the school late and found the parking lot full, as usual, but there were no police cars in sight. The parking lot was small and was always full for any event, even small events. People parked on the side streets, annoying many residents. We parked on a street behind the school and walked to the gym.

We had to take a roundabout route to the gym because of a creek and a briar patch between the school and the creek. Enterprising students had cut a crude path through the maze of thorn bushes to avoid walking all the way around. After crossing the pedestrian bridge over the creek Connie said. "Let's take the path… it's shorter. You have a light, don't you?"

"Yeah, I always carry my pen light. Aren't you afraid of scratching your legs or tearing your dress?"

"I'll keep close; lead the way."

"Take my hand. The path is wet and slippery." I chuckled. "I also have a first aid kit, just in case. Always prepared, that's the Boy Scout motto."

"Is this an excuse to hold my hand?"

"Like I said *always* prepared… and this is your idea, dear. I will take advantage of every opportunity. I am looking forward to stealing a kiss from you before this is all over."

"Aren't you afraid Kathy, or one of your other girlfriends, will be jealous?"

"I'll kiss her too." I laughed. "She was as sweet as you, I think… but I will have to get another sample to be sure… to make it scientific." I chuckled. "And I still owe Elie."

"Ooh, aren't we getting bold." She giggled.

She grabbed my arm as her sneakers slipped on the fall detritus. "Boy this path *is* slippery. My shoes don't have any grip."

"Those shoes aren't made for…"

"*AAaaaiieee! Rrooaarrr!*" Dark shadows jumped from the bushes beside the path.

Connie leaped and tried to grab me, but she stumbled over bushes beside the path and fell into the briars.

Two dark figures ran away up the path, laughing and screaming. I was tempted to give chase, but Connie was screaming horribly.

I charged in among the thorny briars. My light fell on a frightening scene. Connie had fallen into what must have been the thickest patch of thorny vines and they were wrapped around her. She was flailing and struggling, making matters worse.

"Oh God, Oh God something's biting me, Michael. Aeee! Help. Get it off me. Oh God. It's biting." I rushed to help her. I hoped, vainly, that someone would hear her and come to help. The situation appeared hopeless.

We were in a panic as I shined the light on her legs. She was struggling and I yelled, "Connie, Connie, stop struggling. You're making it worse. You're tangled in the vines." I wrapped my arms around her and held her tight. "Connie, you have to be still. Stop fighting."

"Oh, oh. It hurts. Michael, get them off." She grabbed my neck, held on and sobbed on my shoulder. But she became calm, and she was able to hold the light while I cut the vines around her ankles with my scout knife. She was shaking and moaning in pain with every move.

"Michael, forget those down there. Get these… around my backside… and… up here." She pulled her skirt up to reveal the vines wrapped around her waist and between her legs. They were tangled in her underwear, and they were wrapped tight. I could not see if there was blood in the dull light. I was reluctant to touch her, and she growled through gritted teeth, "Michael, don't be shy now. Get the damn things off. Oh, oh, they hurt so. *Do something… now! Please!*"

I lifted the vines, cut them and pulled them away from her buttocks, groin and thighs. I lifted her up to sit on my shoulder as I cut the vines from her ankles.

"Help me out of here, Michael." She cried. "Oh my God it hurts. I don't think I can walk, I lost my shoes."

"Sit on my shoulder. I'll carry you."

"Are you sure you can lift, me... *aaiheee*..." She wrapped her arms around my head as I carried her down to the path along the creek and out to the school yard behind the gym.

I put her down by the side doors to the gym. I was shocked by the amount of blood from wounds on her arms and legs; the nastiest one was on the inside of her thigh. "This looks bad." I clamped my hand over the wound. "I have to wrap this. It is more than a scratch." I used a Carlisle dressing from my medical pack and wrapped it around her leg. Some of the wounds on her arms were bleeding seriously. I used most of the patches in my pack to cover them and wrap dressings around her arms. "Can you walk? We can get to the locker room through these doors. I'll get Miss Ketterman. You need to go to the hospital."

"There's a phone in the locker room. I'll call Daddy. He can take me to the base hospital."

I helped her up and as we entered, we met girls coming from the locker room. They stared at the blood dripping from Connie's arms and legs.

"*Run and get Miss Ketterman, now! Hurry!*" I bellowed. I am sure I sounded mad; I was frantic and scared. The girls squealed and ran off and I hoped they did what I asked. I took Connie into the locker room. She called her father and said he would come to pick her up and take her to the hospital at the naval base; it was closer than the Harrisburg Hospital. Miss Ketterman, the school nurse, came and chased me out of the girl's locker room and tended to Connie's wounds.

I went to the boys' locker room to care for the cuts all over my hands. Blood was all over my shirt and coat. I decided I couldn't stay for the dance like that. I was sure that Connie was in good hands, but I poked my head into the girl's room to make sure and was met with screams to *get out.*

As I left the school by the side door, I met boys coming from the dance in the Gymnasium and when they asked me about the blood on my shirt I quibbled and mumbled some lame story about cutting myself on a thorn bush and then left hastily rather than answer more questions; I did not mention Connie.

I tried to call Connie's home late that evening and again Saturday morning, but I did not get an answer. I recalled that she said her family was going to Seattle for Thanksgiving weekend. I worried that she would be alright. I told my mother and father about Connie getting all cut up in the thorn bushes but did not tell them how I helped her.

I asked Dad on Sunday if he had seen Commander McCormick at the legion and he said they left early Saturday for Seattle, so I assumed Connie would be ok if they went to Seattle on schedule. I breathed a little easier.

CHAPTER 13

I arrived at school Monday morning expecting questions about Friday night, but the hallways were quiet. No one said anything about Connie, indeed no one spoke to me at all. Now you might ask why I did not wonder about that, but I had always been content to be unnoticed and I found it easy to revert to old habits and sit at the back of the classrooms *hoping* the teacher would ignore me. Being ignored did not make me uncomfortable in the least, I was used to that, and even preferred it. The moments that I was in the lime light were enjoyable, in the moment, but I was relieved when they were past and I could return to my shell. On this day I was relieved that I did not have to explain about Friday evening.

Not being overly sports minded, junior baseball being a glaring exception, it did not occur to me until late in the afternoon that the class was unusually quiet given the awesome win over arch rival York High, not to mention the riot afterward. When I finally thought about it, I began to notice that students became very quiet when I came near. In spite of my occasional new found popularity, I was not really a social person, jumping into conversations. I either avoided crowds or was content to hang around the fringes; again, unnoticed.

The day passed quickly and as I sat in the truck in the evening waiting for the parking lot to empty, I was thinking about the day, and I had a nagging feeling something was off. Something about the day gnawed at the edges of my conscience.

The traffic cleared and I headed for home.

On Tuesday I found graffiti scrawled across my locker door. *Slasher Mike* and *Mike the knife. That* got my attention. Shocked, I looked around and yelled, "What's this? Who put this here?"

No one answered and everyone began to move off... slink off with averted eyes.

"Who messed with my locker?" I shouted. A girl nearby slammed her locker door and ran off. I recognized her as the junior classman who went for Miss Ketterman on Friday. I was left alone in an empty hallway, conscious of the silence and pondering the graffiti.

I asked Mister Clayton, the custodian, if he had any paint remover so I could clean the locker. He growled that his supplies were not for students. Then as he was shuffling away, he muttered, "You made your bed boy. You can sleep in it."

What did he say? What did he mean by that? Does he think I messed up my locker? What the heck? Is Clayton nuts? Why do I wonder? It was his crazy idea to plant those stupid thorn bushes... to keep kids from cutting through there.

I used my pen knife to scrape off the marks. It all came off easy enough, although it left scratches. Clayton might growl about that but most of the lockers had scratches and dents. They all needed painting or replacing.

By noon I was more aware of people avoiding me and I began to pay more attention to what was happening. I saw cautious looks and when I looked at someone who was staring at me, they looked away hastily.

I arrived in English literature class and dropped off a book report at Miss Wilson's desk. "What is this? Another self-righteous rant about current events?" She complained.

"It's a book report on the life of Andrew Jackson, like you asked."

"I'll bet you enjoyed reading about a man who was a bully?"

"Jackson was an American hero and a president."

"He was notable for his bullying."

I shrugged. "Yeah, he did have a temper."

"A man after your own heart."

"Not really. He was a slave owner, and he oppressed the Indians." I was puzzled by her hostility. That had not reared its head for some time. "The Indian removal act was passed by him."

She gave me an annoyed look. "*You* don't see your conduct as bullying?"

"What conduct? I've never bullied anyone."

"You don't think what you did to Miss McCormick was bullying?" That got my attention. "What I did to… what are you talking about?"

"Friday at the dance, you dragged her all cut and bleeding into the locker room."

"I did not drag her into the locker room, Miss Wilson. I helped her because she couldn't walk."

"No thanks to you and your knife. Are you taking McCaskey's place… since you chased him and his brother out of town?"

I protested. "What the he… heck are you talking about?"

My irritation must have showed, as her mood abruptly changed, her eyes widened and I saw fear on her face. With forced politeness, she said, "You can take your seat now Mister Hunter."

"What do you mean taking McCaskey's place? And bullying Connie?" I leaned against her desk. I must have loomed because she pushed her chair back, away from the desk, and stood up.

She was nervous and she looked as if she wanted to run. Her hands were shaking, and she clinched them tightly in front of her. She meekly said, "Please, Michael, take your seat. I will read your report. Thank you for your promptness."

I was wary of the change and stepped back. She ignored me for the rest of the day. However, others didn't. In the hallways I saw people look at me and mutter, "Shame!", "Disgraceful", or 'Fiend". Miss Wilson's name was mentioned several times. Someone saw the encounter that morning and it apparently made the rounds of the school.

Eleanor and Carol approached me at my locker. "I never thought you would do something like this. You were always so quiet and polite." Eleanor said. "I don't know what's gotten into you. You've changed since… since last year and not for the better."

"What…?" My mind was in a muddle.

"I am disappointed in you, Michael. You should be ashamed of yourself." Carol chimed in.

"Ashamed? For what?" I groaned, "I have not done anything to be ashamed of."

"Michael, you need help." They scurried off without an explanation. I stood there shaking wondering what they were talking about. What's got everyone so upset? Miss Wilson mentioned Connie.

I stood by my locker watching students scurry past and now I could see they were avoiding me, keeping to the far side of the hallway. They were obviously talking about me. I saw many sneakily look and point at me. They looked away quickly when I looked at them. What do they think I did? I thought about the writing on the locker and Wilson's reference to a knife and Connie. I finally began to put it all together. Boy; am I slow… dense as a doorknob. That's what I get for not paying attention.

Good God they think I cut Connie. How could they think that? I did not know whether to cry or scream. I needed someone to talk to me, but the halls were suddenly empty.

Rumors and gossip were going around about me and Connie, and people were filling in the blanks with their imagination. That is what I get for being quiet.

When I went to my truck I found, to my horror, that someone had scratched the paint on the doors and the hood. *Fiend, bully boy, Mike the knife, rapist, pervert,* was scrawled all over. I searched the empty school yard and parking lot but there were no likely suspects in sight.

I fumed as I drove home. I did not want Mom or Dad to see the mess. They would not be home for a while; so, I found paint in the garage and wiped it on the damage with a sponge until I was satisfied that the marks were covered up. It was not perfect but the well-ordered red and yellow flames I had carefully painted around the edge of the engine compartment and fenders now spread extravagantly, and crudely, over the hood and doors. The paint was rough, but the scratches were not visible.

I waited in front of the school early Wednesday morning as students made wide detours around me. I saw Eleanor arrive with Carol and I stood in front of them. They did not even look me in the face as they tried to go around me. I stepped in front of them and blocked their path. Eleanor finally made eye contact.

"Michael, get out of the way."

"No! Not until you explain to me what is going on."

"Michael. If you don't know…"

"Let's cut the innuendo and hogwash." She looked frightened and I mellowed my tone. "Tell me what you think I have done that calls for all this… this stuff. Someone scratched my truck… after they messed up my locker. I want some answers."

"I am sorry about your truck." Eleanor said. "I did not have anything to do with that…"

"Stop avoiding the subject, Eleanor. Tell me what's going on."

She backed up. "You don't have to yell, Michael."

"How else can I get someone to talk *to* me instead of avoiding me?"

"Everyone knows… or, uh… thinks you cut Connie and… and, uh, rap… hurt her." She averted her eyes looking frightened.

I caught her hesitation. *"Rape? Who told you that?"*

"Several students, about six or seven saw all the blood all over her legs and… and on her underwear. And some boys saw you, uh… at the dance… with blood all over you… and they said you ran away. The girls said she had been cut in the, uh… her, uh, private parts." Carol was distraught. "They say you slashed her with a knife because… because she would not give in to you… give you…" She stopped, looking around, nervous and frightened.

"No. No. *That is a lie.*" I was not keeping my voice down and a crowd was gathering. *"Who is saying that?"* I was nervous and scared now at hearing this. *"No. That isn't what happened.* We tried to cut through the briar patch. Some kids jumped up and frightened us. Connie fell into the bushes and was caught in the vines. I cut the vines to help her. The briars were around her legs and some of them cut deep. There was a lot of blood. I had to put a dressing on her leg."

"Michael, we've all brushed against those briars. They don't cause that much damage."

"You've *brushed* against them… Connie fell into the *middle* of the damn bushes. The vines were wrapped around her legs and… her rump. It was dark and she thought she was being bitten… she was frightened and struggling and that caused them to cut deeper…"

"Michael Hunter what are you doing here?" Mister Martin, the Principal came out accompanied by coach Cord and Mister Trestler, the math teacher and senior class advisor, and other teachers.

"I am trying to find out what is going on…"

"We are going to do an investigation and we will find out the truth. In the meantime you should go home."

"Go home! Why? I haven't done anything. Anyway, how can you do an investigation without *talking to me?"* My voice was rising.

"We will determine that in due…"

"I'm being punished in the meantime. *What ever happened to innocent until proven guilty?*"

"If you are so innocent why isn't Connie here this week?" Miss Wilson said, "It's obvious she is afraid of you."

"*You. You* are probably the one spreading gossip… spreading lies. We all know you…"

"Stop, Michael." Martin commanded, "I will not allow you to attack the teachers… or students. You are obviously upset… with all this yelling and screaming. Go home. Now!"

"No! Connie is not here because she and her family went to a reunion in Washington State this week. It's a family tradition." I looked at Eleanor and pointed at her. "*You* should know that. I know she told you about it." She appeared hesitant but nodded. "Someone is spreading stories." I looked at Miss Wilson.

"That is enough. I told you not to talk about the teachers." Martin was getting mad. "You need to leave, right now! Or I will make your suspension for longer than a day. Perhaps you would like it to be permanent."

"Suspension. Why am I being suspended? I haven't done anything." My head was going crazy. I tried to keep from whining… to stop screaming.

"We will decide that. Take your books and get off school property at once or you will be removed." Mister Cord and Martin moved toward me, and I backed away. I dumped my books on the roadway. "Pick those books up Michael or I *will* suspend you indefinitely."

"You do that, *Mister* Martin." I spoke through tears. "You are all a bunch of hypocrites and liars. I don't think you can teach me anything useful." I walked away trying to hide my tears. I heard Eleanor call out, but I kept walking. At the truck, I tossed the empty bag in the back and sat on the running board crying. I was angry and scared.

"Michael." Mister Trestler's voice startled me. I hastily wiped the tears away and jumped into the truck before he could see me. When he called out again, I started the truck and the straight exhaust pipes made such a racket that they drowned him out. After a couple of clumsy attempts, I got the truck into gear and roared out of the parking lot.

I had a hard time seeing the road through tears and had to stop along the road while I dried my eyes and cleared my vision.

How can they think I would do that to Connie? Or to anyone. Who is telling stories? Wilson? Those girls from the locker room? It must have been them. They saw all the blood and made up stories. I left the dance too quick without explaining anything… and I had blood all over my shirt. I *did* rush out.

Mom and Dad were not home, and I rambled around trying to be calm. I tried reading something but could not concentrate. My mind was filled with confusion, and I could not think.

I needed to be alone, and I decided to go sailing, even though it was November and very cold. My plans developed as I gathered things that I would need to stay warm. The activity distracted me from thinking about the school and the wild stories. I gathered a hammock, sleeping bag, pup tent, and fishing rod. I thought I could camp on one of the islands… maybe Tanner's Island; that was big and empty.

I wrote a note giving a sketchy description of the week and my suspension. I explained that I needed to be by myself for a while to think. To be truthful, I did not want to listen to Mom's lectures, but I did not mention *that* in my note.

As I loaded the truck, I thought maybe I should take something to read. Maybe a good fiction would help take my mind off my problems... if I could get myself to read it. I grabbed a book that appeared interesting. It was one of my mother's and I knew we both enjoyed adventure stories and I thought the title, *Treasures*, sounded adventurous. It would be perfect for an adventure on the river. I did not look inside and hastily wrapped it in wax paper and stuffed it in my haversack.

I loaded the boat into the back of the truck and hauled it down to the firemen's ramp in York Landing. I rigged the sprit sail and set out with no thought to where I was going. I sailed up the river for a while enjoying the quiet. It was cold and it would get colder by evening, so I turned back near Fall Island. I trolled a fishing line from the boat and caught two small fish. It was past noon when I set up camp on Tanner Island.

Tanner Island was a privately owned island. There were a couple of abandoned barns, but no one lived on the island. There were rumors that a new power plant was to be built there, a nuclear power plant. I set up camp near one of the barns, cleaned and cooked the fish.

I found a game trail and set up a snare. I rigged my pup tent halves into a lean-to between two trees, hung my hammock and sat back to relax with the fire warming my shelter. I took out the book and felt disappointed to discover that it was a book of bible verses. I tossed the book down in disgust, but after sitting bored for a half hour I picked it up and began paging through it.

The book had verses arranged by topic. I read about the first sin, the serpent and his deception, telling the woman that God was lying. I thought that was a fable. I read the story of Cain and Abel and noted God's warning to Cain about sin lying at the door and that he must master it. That reminded me of something Mom had said. I randomly paged through the book skimming over various passages.

I checked my snare; I had caught a rabbit. I skinned and cleaned that and while that cooked, I made some bannock bread with flour that I brought from the kitchen. Afterward, I sat back in the hammock and continued reading in the book by the light of a camp lantern.

"Do not judge so that you will not be judged. For in the way you judge, you will be judged; and by your standard of measure, it will be measured to you" and "He who is without sin among you, let him be the first to throw a stone at her."

I thought these verses applied very well to the people at school. I read it again. "He who is without sin among you let him be the first to throw a stone." Yes! I thought. Maybe I should show this to my so-called friends and fellow students… not to mention the teachers.

I read about Christ dying for sins and that everyone has sinned and needed to repent. I did not see that I had anything to repent of; I did not sin, and I ignored the part that said *all* have sinned. That *couldn't* apply to me. I ignored things that made me uncomfortable like, "If we say that we have no sin, we are deceiving ourselves and the truth is not in us."

I reasoned that it was not *me* who was in the wrong. It was everyone else, not me! It is the people making the gossip and the school leaders who needed to repent. I tried very hard to excuse myself. I went to sleep… or tried to sleep with those thoughts in my head.

I spent Thursday reading and hiking and sailing around the island while thinking about the mess at school. I caught some more fish and snared another rabbit and occasionally perused the book looking for verses that supported my view.

I had only planned to be gone for one night, but I became engrossed in the book and my thoughts, and it became dark very quickly. I decided to wait until Friday morning. I forgot that it was Thanksgiving and Mom was preparing dinner… it would be our first thanksgiving since my brother, Andy, left for the Naval Academy.

Early the next morning I sailed back to York Landing after a breakfast of fish and finishing the bannock bread.

Mom met me as I parked beside the garage. Dad's car was not there. "Michael Hunter, where have you been?" She was mad. "We have been worried sick. You missed thanksgiving dinner, and your father has been running around looking for you."

"I left a note."

"Oh yes! Your note said that you had been expelled from school and you wanted to be alone for a while. As if that was going to make us feel better. You said you were going out on the river; *in November*. Michael, no one goes out on the river in the winter."

"Yeah, it was pretty quiet, and cold." I laughed. "But I stayed warm." I tried to be lighthearted but that was like throwing gas on a fire.

"This is *not* funny young man. What do you mean you were expelled? How did that happen?" I explained about the week and Wednesday morning's confrontation. She was not impressed. "Michael, I have warned you that your temper was going to get you in trouble."

"But it wasn't my fault. It's not fair. Everyone is convicting me without even trying to find out the truth. It's a lynch mob."

"Ok, ok. We'll go Monday morning and straighten this out."

"Connie should be back by then."

"Your father is out with men from the legion. They were talking about calling the firemen to go out looking for you on the river after someone mentioned seeing your truck in York Landing. I should call the legion or the firehall and tell them you are home."

She called the fire hall, but they said Dad was not there. She worried out loud that he and the men had gone out on the river, so she called the legion. When she hung up the phone she had a puzzled look.

"What's wrong, Mom?"

"I—I don't know. That was the strangest conversation. It was like they didn't want to talk to me. Rebekah, the secretary, said that no one was looking for you. You father is in some meeting about a problem that came up. Rebekah sounded hostile. She was stingy with details and then just hung up."

Mom prepared a dinner of the abundant leftovers from the day before… a late thanksgiving dinner. She wondered what was keeping Dad as she, Charlie and I ate without him.

I was in the rec room in the basement when I heard a car come into the driveway. I jumped when the door slammed upstairs, and my father began yelling. Mom sounded upset as she asked him to calm down. My chest went tight as I listened. He sounded very mad... he was swearing... a lot. The way he said my name disturbed me... the way it was said. I hesitated on the stairs but continued upward. I came out of the basement and was almost bowled over as Mom rushed by with a wet cloth.

"Look out, Michael. Don't get in the way. I have to look after your father."

"What happened? Was there an accident?" I spoke.

"No, there was no accident." Dad growled around the cloth covering his face. One eye was not covered, and he had it fixed on me. "What happened at that dance, boy and don't lie?"

"I told you some children frightened Connie and she fell in the thorn bushes at the school. I helped her get out and bandaged a cut."

"What happened in the bushes?"

"Nothing happened. Like I said she was tangled in the briars, and I had to cut the vines from around her legs."

"What else? Did you take advantage of her? Touch her, attack her?" His voice was rising. He was obviously drunk, but I had never seen him like this before and apparently, from the worried look on Mom's face, and her repeated pleas for him to calm down, neither had she.

"Attacked her? What do you mean attack her? No, I didn't attack her." I hesitated. "I had to touch her to get the vines off her."

"You *had* to touch her." He mocked. "You took advantage of her and molested her." It was an accusation, not a question.

"I did *not* molest her!"

"Don't lie to me, you... you pervert!"

"James, stop! Don't talk like that."

He stood up and screamed. *"Don't talk like what?* I have been attacked by my friends because my son is a pervert."

"*I am not a pervert!* I did not do anything to Connie. I don't know what kind of lies you are hearing but they are rumors started by kids at school. *They are lies. I am telling you...*" I stood up yelling. He rushed around the table, and I fled from the kitchen, scared.

"Don't you use that tone with me, boy! Don't you turn your back on me! *Come back here!*"

I ignored him and headed for my bedroom to get away. He caught me in the hallway.

"*Jim! Wait! Stop!*" Mom cried.

I tried to pull away and Dad lashed out and smacked me across the face. I fell, stunned.

Mom screamed and rushed to intervene. She grabbed at Dad. "Jim, for God's sake stop! What are you doing? He's your son."

Dad pushed her away and she fell down knocking over a table in the hallway. He did not seem to notice. I cowered in a corner, covering my head as Dad hovered over me.

Charlie came to help Mom and yelled at Dad. But he was in a blind drunken rage, and he was not hearing. I half crawled and half ran as I retreated into the bedroom, but he pushed through the door and cornered me. He slapped me as I covered my head and protested. *"Now we know truth. You never cared about me. You hate me because I am not like Andy... or Charlie. You believe stupid rumors, but you are nothing but a stupid drunk and a bigger hypocrite than those men at the church you talk about."*

Charlie screamed at him from the hall. *"Dad, stop. You hurt Mom!"*

Through my tears I screamed. *"What are you going to do, Dad? Beat me up? And then what? Beat up Mom and Charlie?"*

Dad looked from me to Mom and Charlie. He hesitated and appeared confused. He backed away from me shaking his head. A confused look; a look of dismay came over his face. He stared at his shaking hands and his mouth moved wordlessly. He made a choking sound, turned and fled down the hall past Mom and Charlie. The car roared out of the driveway.

Mom rushed to me and took me in her arms, clutching me to her breast, and crying. I tried to pull away, but she would not let go. "Oh God, I'm so sorry, Michael. Oh Lord, forgive us. I'm sorry. I believe you. I do believe you."

Mom took Charlie to his room because he was upset and crying. She returned and sat on my bed, gently talking. She held me for a long time, and I put my arms around her and held onto her as she prayed softly. I fell asleep listening to her prayer.

Hours had passed when I woke up. The house was quiet. I cautiously opened my bedroom door. I did not see anyone, but I thought

I heard voices from my parents' bedroom. I slipped out of my bedroom and went to the bathroom. The bruise where Dad hit me throbbed. I washed my face, sweeping the water over my head, and held a cold wet cloth on the bruise.

I was hungry and as I moved down the hallway past my parents' bedroom, I heard voices again. But it was just one voice; Mom's. The door was slightly open, and I paused to listen.

She was talking in a low voice and crying. I felt sick hearing her cry like that. I became choked up. Mom cried at sad movies, but this was different… there was desperation to her voice that I never heard before. I cautiously pushed the door open and stopped when I realized she was praying.

She pleaded, "Lord Jesus help Michael. Look out for him. We have failed him, but I know you will not. He needs you now more than ever. Please, Lord, look after my son and show him the way… the right way. I love him so and I know you love him.

"And Lord, watch over my husband, James. You know his heart and that he is a good man, and I love him so much. I know he did not mean the things he said, or the things he did. Rebuke Satan and don't let him have his way with Jimmie, or with our family. Have *your* way. And I know he loves Michael. He is hurting now and his friends, his earthly friends, have let him down, but I know you never let your children down. Lift him up. Restore him, and bring him home safely, and forgive him."

I felt embarrassed that I was listening to a private conversation. I could not bear to listen any longer and I pulled the door shut.

My stomach was queasy. I was not sure if it was hunger or from listening to Mom, but I looked for something to eat anyway.

I took a bottle of milk from the fridge and cut a piece of the pumpkin pie. I started to sit in Dad's chair, like I usually did when Dad was not there. I hesitated, a stupid uneasiness running through my head. Then I shrugged and sat down, pondering the silliness of the thought.

We kids have been in the habit of sitting in Dad's place when he is not home. He always joked about us trying to usurp his place. It was never a big deal, *so why now?* I suspected there was an answer to that, but I didn't dwell on it.

I finished the pie and became aware of Mom leaning against the door frame, watching me. I looked at her and felt warm inside.

"Can I get you anything, Michael?"

"No. I've got all I need right now. Thank you." I looked at her tear stained face. I felt an overwhelming love for her and whispered softly. "Thank You."

She had a look on her face, almost a smile as she answered softly. "You're welcome." She sat down close to me, watching me quietly. The love in her eyes made me look away, and a tear came to my eye.

"Did God answer your prayer?" I spoke.

"Yes." She said confidently.

She was serious. I spoke. "I wish I had your faith."

"You can. He always listens… and he always answers."

I answered bitterly. "Yeah. Well, I know I don't have to worry about God believing me. He knows everything. Doesn't He? He knows the truth, that I did not do the things you…" I looked away. "Dad… or everyone, thinks I did."

"We messed up, your dad and me."

"I don't think you messed up. You're perfect." I whispered as I rubbed the bruise on my face.

"Oh, I don't know about that, but thank you." She kissed me. "He is hurting, Michael and he's scared."

"Dad, Scared?" I scoffed. "That's hard to believe. Him, hurting? Maybe not as much as me."

She touched the bruise. "This is bad, but it is only on the outside. It will heal. The hurt he feels, and the hurt I know you feel now is on the inside… that will take more time to heal. Believe me he is hurting. Maybe even more than you, as hard as you may find that to believe. He is." She said softly.

Mom's plea moved me. I could not think of anything to say; but she was frightened. I have never seen her so worried and that bothered me.

"I—I'm sure he'll be ok, Mom." I touched her hand. She smiled warmly.

CHAPTER 14

Dad did not come home that night and I slept late on Saturday morning. Mom was already up, and she was making breakfast when I came to the kitchen.

"Dad's not home?"

She set a bowl of cereal in front of me and touched my shoulder. "No and I am worried."

"Maybe he's at the legion."

She sat down with a cup of tea. "He would not spend all night there. It closes at two. I called there already, and they would not tell me anything." She looked troubled.

"What?"

"They were abrupt and sounded hostile… as if they did not want to talk to me. I don't understand; they hung up when I asked what was going on."

I ate slowly and suggested. "Maybe you should go and talk to them."

"I was thinking that. Can you drive me?"

"Sure."

We arrived at the legion and walked into the banquet hall where men and women were preparing for the annual Thanksgiving Dinner and dance that night. The cook, Ella stared at Mom and said brusquely. "What are *you* doing here?" She looked at me and added, "Why did you bring *him*?"

"I *am* a member here Ella. Why shouldn't I be here? After all, we have the big thanksgiving dinner tonight, don't we? My son offered to drive me. Why shouldn't he be here?"

"I am surprised you would show your face after what he did." She sneered.

Some people tried to block our way, but Mom just pushed past them. "Are you going to beat me up like you did my husband?" They moved aside. "Tell me. Why shouldn't my son be here?"

"We don't want him here, especially after what he did." Mat Kowalski said. "I am surprised he is still running loose."

"*Just what is it you think Michael has done?*" Mom's voice rose ominously as she lifted her head and looked down her nose at the Chef. I don't know how she did that... look *down* her nose considering the big man towered over her diminutive frame. He backed away.

"Officer Kane was here. He told us about the dance Friday night." Ella said, "He is looking for this pervert."

People came from the office and joined the gathering crowd. They echoed Ella's question. "What is he doing here?"

I said, "Who is this Officer Kane and why is he looking for me? Why hasn't he come to the house... or to the school? I was at home and at school most of this week."

"That's a good question." Mom said, "The police know where we live."

"What does Officer Kane claim I have done?" I spoke.

"It's all over the district. The kids came home from school with the horrible news. How you slashed that McCormick girl with a knife. She had to go to the hospital. We heard she almost died." Kowalski snarled, "We heard you cut her in the…"

"In the crotch." Ella snarled.

"Maybe I should cut you like you cut her." Mat flashed a kitchen knife. "Give you a dose of your own medicine."

"You will not be cutting my son, Mathew Kowalski… or anyone else." Mom stepped in front of him, and he backed away again under her glare.

Rebekah Leeder, the secretary murmured, "My daughter came home and said there was blood all over the locker room. Connie was cut in her private parts by your pervert son."

The big cook acted like she was going to hit my mother. I thought I would have to protect Mom, but she faced Ella and growled, *"Don't you dare threaten my son, Ella!* You are so stupid. You are *all* so stupid. *If* my son had attacked Connie, don't you think that Ian and Elizabeth would have done something about that? Do you really believe they would have gone off on vacation with Connie and done nothing?" Ella looked away, uneasy.

Rebekah and Ella exchanged nervous looks. "I—I Well, uh, no I guess not." Rebekah said petulantly, "Maybe Connie was too frightened."

"Even if Connie were frightened, do you think her father would have been?" I spoke. Mat was staring at the floor. "Mister Kowalski, if Jennifer had been attacked would you let a day go by without doing something to catch the person who did it? Would you just go off on vacation as if nothing happened?"

"Of course not. I would be looking for the..." Kowalski put the knife down. "But Billie Kane said... he seemed certain that you had done it. I don't know why he hasn't arrested you. It has been a week."

Someone in the crowd said that I had been missing, apparently hiding out on the river. They pointed out that my father had come to get help to look for me.

I spoke. "I was only on the river Wednesday to Friday morning... I was home all last weekend and in school Monday to Wednesday morning, and no one called the police." I was silent for a moment and when no one spoke I explained. "Connie fell in the thorn bushes, and I cut the vines to help her get out. I took her to the girls' locker room. Some kids saw the blood and let their imagination run wild." I paused, "I guess I was stupid to leave so quickly like I did. But I was afraid of embarrassing Connie. I guess I just made it worse."

"Yes, and you beat up on Jimmy when he asked for help." My mother growled. "You are *supposed* to be our friends. We have been members for years and Jimmy was post commander last year. He is the post finance officer for God's sake. And he has often helped *all* of you at some point or other. And you turned on him like a pack of wolves." She scoffed, "Some friends you are."

"Who the heck is Officer Kane anyway?" I said, "I never heard of him."

"Billy Kane played for the football team a couple of years ago." Kowalski said.

"Oh, yeah. Wait! Now I remember, he was friends with Jimmie McCaskey... and I think I remember him being part of his gang when they were younger. He was on the River Road when we fought with them a couple of years ago." I said, "That would explain a lot." I paused. "Is Martha Kane his sister?"

"His cousin." Ella said, "Why?"

I laughed. "Martha is the biggest gossip in the senior class. She pals around with Miss Wilson and Miss Gleeson, two of the biggest gossips, and bigots, in the school."

"Michael, you should not talk like that about the teachers." Mom admonished me.

"I am just saying. It's a known fact… Martha is the teachers' pet, and she carries tales. She has been known to inflate stories to impress her teachers and they repeat the tales."

Hanna said, "I know Wilson and Gleeson. They go to my church. They are talkers, and they are very opinionated."

"And racist." I muttered.

"Michael!" Mom warned.

More legion members arrived, and they listened while I told them about the Friday night and answered questions. "I am not trying to make myself out a hero. I just did what I could to help her. Maybe if I explained things then, it would not have gotten out of hand. The guys tell stories as much as the, uh… Martha… and she is not alone in that. I was afraid they would twist things around, so I did not tell them anything. Connie was already embarrassed enough."

Dale Cummins, the current commander, said, "Perhaps we *have* been hasty."

"You think?" I muttered under my breath, which brought a poke in the ribs from mom, and a sharp look.

Cummins added. "We should wait and talk to Ian and Elizabeth…. and Connie. They will be back on Sunday."

John Springer the master at arms suggested, "Maybe we should pass the word around to our members, to stop talking and spreading rumors… and to other service clubs."

Mom said, "Jimmy came home Friday night, and he was… well, he was drunk and irrational. He got in a terrible row with Michael and stormed out of the house. I have not seen him since. Will you help me find him?"

The meeting broke up with some offering apologies, but others still doubtful and apparently not convinced. However, they conceded that they would reserve judgement; until they heard from Connie, and they promised to keep an eye out for my dad.

After a light lunch, Mom and I drove around to some of Dad's usual haunts. We did not stay long because we got hard looks and coarse comments when people learned who I was. After a couple of stops I stayed in the truck. However, Mom said she still met with suspicious looks and hostility when she introduced herself.

"I cannot believe that story has circulated so wide and so quickly. How do so many people know us?" I lamented.

"Your father is well known in the township. Remember he was legion Commander last year and he is active… prominent in little league sports. He writes for the local paper occasionally, not to mention many letters to the Mechanicsburg Journal and the Patriot."

I spoke. "Yeah, and McCaskey has many *friends*. I'll bet Billy Kane has been busy making the rounds. John and Mac are probably looking for revenge and they are enjoying this."

We stopped at Collins garage to fill the gas tank. While Collin's attendant, Rodney, pumped the gas I went inside.

"Hello Mister Collins. I'm sorry I did not come in today. Mom and I have been looking for Dad. We had some trouble at home, and he has not been home all night. I was wondering if you might have seen him."

"Your dad stopped for gas this morning, early and then headed for the 84 ramp. He seemed distracted and in a hurry. I think he may have been drinking. But I am not sure."

"Oh ok. I'll try to be here on Monday."

"Don't bother, Michael. I don't think I'll be needing you anymore."

"Anymore?" I was puzzled. "Am I being fired?"

He looked at the floor uncomfortably. "Yeah, I guess you could say that."

"Why?" I saw CC watching from the office. She ducked inside when I looked at her. "Is there a problem, Mister Collins?"

"Well, I've been hearing things… from school. An officer was here asking about you. He said some things that trouble me."

"You heard some things from school and this officer told you *some things*. So, you believe rumors and gossip."

"It sounds like more than gossip to me Michael." He sounded indignant. "CC told me what happened at the school. I don't need your sort around here, scaring customers."

"My sort?" I was seething. "You talk about injustice and prejudice, but you have no problem swallowing BS. Aren't you being hypocritical?"

Mom came and touched my arm. "Michael, let it go."

"Is it BS Michael? You have a reputation in the district for fighting. I remember the fight you had with Mac and his gang… and CC told me about his brother. You seem to be a violent person. I can't have you around the customers… or CC."

"I was in two fights, and that was last year."

"What about the incident at the ball game?"

"Yeah, like I started that." I rolled my eyes. "That was hardly a fight and the one at school was at Coach Cord and Principal Martin's insistence… and I rescued your niece from that gang." I glanced toward the office. "Would you rather I had done nothing… like everyone else?" CC remained out of sight, but I knew she was listening. "I haven't been in any other fights, not even an argument. A bunch of rumors come out of the school and the whole township goes nuts. I don't think I *want* to work for you. You are as bad as those hypocrites at school. That's what you all are… hypocrites." I snarled and abruptly walked out.

CC called out. "You have to pay for the gas, Michael."

Mom began to root in her bag, but I pulled a five-dollar bill from my pocket, crumpled it in a ball and tossed it on the floor at her feet. "Keep the change." I stormed out.

"Michael!" I stopped. Mom looked sadly from me to CC. I thought Mom wanted to apologize. CC had her hands over her mouth, her eyes wide. Mom did not say anything as we drove home.

"If Dad took 84 going south, he must have wanted to get as far from people who knew him as he could." I said finally.

"He may go to the legion in York."

Sunday morning, Mom asked me to drive her to church since Dad was not home yet and had not been found.

I parked and we walked to the front door. People standing out front stared at us and huddled in close groups watching us.

"You have a lot of nerve, Anne, coming here this morning with *him*." Hellen Grange sneered as we entered the vestibule of the church.

"This is God's house, and I am sure everyone is welcome."

"*He* isn't." She jerked her chin toward me. "He is *not* welcome after what he did to that girl."

I was about to speak but Mom poked me in the ribs. "I don't know where you are getting your information, but it is all lies. If my son was any of those things he would be in the jail now. Haven't you heard what our Lord said, 'Do not judge. The way you judge, you will be judged. By your standard it will be measured to you'?"

"You have a lot of nerve coming here quoting scripture, Mrs. Hunter." Sherry, the organist said.

"It's the Lord's word, not mine, Sherri. I think *you* need to read it sometime." Mom glared at the young organist. It was more than a rumor around church that she was fooling around with the pastor. Sherri let out a low gasp, but Mom glared at her and spoke. "Do you follow the Lord or do you just worship with your lips. It seems to me your heart is far from God.

"This is a Church of our Lord Jesus Christ, and you are not acting like his disciples. Jesus accepted everyone. You are all like Pharisees, with the pointing fingers. Wolves in sheep clothing, all meek and docile, until you smell blood. I do not think God is here this morning, so I guess I *am* in the wrong place."

Mom took my arm and ushered me out before I could speak. We sat at a picnic table in the grove near the old church cemetery. "Well at least these people aren't going to judge me." I looked ruefully at the old headstones.

"I am sorry, Michael. That is not right for a church of Christ."

"Yeah, it's like Dad said they are all hypocrites."

"Do you think I am a hypocrite?"

"No. You don't belong with these people. It is better to stay away from churches and religion."

"Michael don't be that way. You can't judge all churches or Christians... or Jesus, by the actions of a few men and women. We are all sinners and only saved by the grace of God, not by our works... or our own goodness.

"The church is the Lord's and even if we do not live up to him, we must still respect it. We have to find a congregation that truly honors him, though. I know that many don't, but we can't turn our back on his church because things do not go our way... it is the same as turning our backs on God."

"Well, I am glad that you have it all figured out. I can't see what there is for me in the church."

"You will never know until you trust in the Lord, Michael. Trust in the Lord, not the church or men. The proverbs say to 'trust in the Lord with all your heart and do not lean on your own understanding, in all your ways acknowledge him and he will direct your path'."

I remembered something like that from that book, *Treasures*.

CHAPTER 15

Monday morning Dad was not home, and Mom paced the floor nervously, muttering prayers. She spilled the milk as she poured it on our cereal and Charlie, and I had to insist on doing it ourselves. The phone rang and she rushed to grab it.

When she tried to hang up, she missed the cradle twice. She spoke. "Your father was at the legion home at Willow until closing. He was not in any shape to drive and Winnie, the night manager, took him home. He apparently left Winnie's early this morning. Winnie thought he was going to head home, but he was not certain."

She no sooner got the phone on the hook than a car pulled into the driveway, and she rushed to the door. It was Ian and Elizabeth.

"Michael, you're here!" I almost spilled the milk as Elizabeth rushed in and hugged me. "Thank you so much for helping Connie last Friday. Your quick action kept a minor cut from becoming serious. Thank you." She looked puzzled as she let go of me. "Shouldn't you be in school? Connie left for school an hour ago."

"I was expelled last Wednesday."

"Expelled!" Ian and Elizabeth gasped together.

I explained what had happened the week before. Their expressions became more incredulous with each detail. Mom began to tell them about our Saturday adventure when a car pulled in to the drive. Mom rushed to the door. "It's Jimmy!" She rushed out and threw her arms around his neck and hugged him tightly. He tried to pry her arms from around his neck but gave up and held her. She hung on and poured out her heart, telling him that she loved him no matter what, that she forgave him, and she was happy to have him home safe. She implored him to come and have something to eat. She took hold of his arm and pulled him into the kitchen. She made him sit and she brought him coffee and a muffin and sat and talked to him. The rest of us sat fidgeting. I felt out of place like when I intruded on Mom's prayers; I was listening in on a private conversation.

Dad listened as Ian told him about taking Connie to the Naval Base hospital from the dance and having her wounds treated. Elizabeth gushed over me as she told us all about what Connie said about me helping her.

Ian was generous with his praise and Elizabeth laughed as she told how I was afraid to touch Connie and that she *demanded* that I *cut the damn vines off* and *don't worry about touching me*. Dad smiled weakly.

While we were talking Elizabeth suddenly blurted. "Oh my God! Connie has gone to school. She is facing those rumors alone. We need to go to the school and straighten this mess out, Ian." She stood up, in a hurry to get moving.

Through it all, Dad sat quietly. He wondered if he should be involved. Mom said. "You *have* to be involved. We are family. We deal with our problems together." I was not ready to forgive him, and Dad and I remained distant with each other.

Ian said to him. "Listen buddy. We all make mistakes, but it is important not to let them get you down. Let's go and deal with this."

I kept my feelings to myself not wanting to upset Mom.

We parked on the side street; Mom and Elizabeth wanted to see the briar patch. We passed over the creek and stopped at the tangle of briars between us and the school.

"The kids like to go through here?" Mom said skeptically.

"My question is why would the custodian leave this mess here with so many kids around?" Ian said.

Dad added. "Someone could hide in here and drag a girl, or a woman, in there." Mom said. "Let's get a closer look. Where is that path?"

Elizabeth looked at Mom's flat soled shoes. "You're the mother of an Eagle Scout, you're wearing flats, and you want to go hiking in the jungle?"

Mom retorted. "I can get both my feet in one of my Eagle Scout's hiking boots. These will have to do. Shall we?" Dad and Ian exchanged amused looks.

"Need I remind you young ladies that it snowed last night, and the ground is slippier than usual?" I spoke. "Slippier than when Connie and I were here."

"That was at night… we have daylight." Elizabeth turned to my mother. "Your young man has a way with words, doesn't he? I don't know if I should be offended or flattered."

"Flattery will get you nowhere, *young* man. The path?" Mom said, pointing at the bushes. I showed them the path and Elizabeth bravely led the way, gingerly making her way along the slippery track.

"Goodness why would any girl want to go through here." Elizabeth looked at me but all I could do was shrug.

Ian muttered. "Kids!"

"That bush looks flattened, Elizabeth." Mom pointed to the demolished bush.

I spoke. "A couple of kids jumped out and scared the crap out of us."

Mom made as if to go down the hill and Elizabeth caught her elbow. *"Oh no you don't."* She laughed. "We'll go around."

We made our way through the tangle to the entrance of the school. As we entered, we heard a great commotion. A large crowd was gathered in the hall near the lockers; Connie was in the middle of the crowd yelling at someone. The only words I could make out at first were stupid, ignorant and few unladylike expletives. We pushed through the crowd to see Connie screaming at Martha.

"How can you be so stupid?"

"I heard what I heard. You said that he attacked…"

"I did not say that! You heard what you wanted to hear. And you carried your lies all around the school! You and those teachers…"

"Miss McCormick, stop." Mister Martin interrupted. "I do not like to hear students talking trash about teachers. You need to calm down and watch your mouth."

"Or what… you'll kick me out of school like you did Michael? Everyone knows that Miss Wilson and Miss Gleeson talk…"

"Connie?" I called. "Don't get yourself in trouble."

"Yes, Sweetheart. Please be quiet." Elizabeth said as she pushed through the crowd.

"*Michael!*" Connie lunged at me and hugged me eagerly. "I can't believe what everyone is saying. They're all crazy."

Ian got Martin's attention. "We need to have a meeting Mister Martin. We have a serious problem here. I hear that rumors and gossip have spread through the district and they started here."

Principal Martin and teachers finally brought some order and sent the students to classes. Martin called for Mister Trestler, Miss Ketterman and some teachers, including Miss Wilson, to meet in the library. Students were called in as the meeting continued all morning with a lot of discussion and debate. Trestler sent for the students who attended in the locker room the night of the dance.

Connie told what happened… in detail. I felt the blood warming my face as I looked around at the walls and fidgeted.

Martha haughtily asserted. "I heard what I heard."

Connie retorted. *"God, I was so scared and in pain I don't even remember what I said.* But I *did not* accuse Michael of cutting me. Michael *did not* cut me. He cut the vines to free me. He *helped* me and bandaged my cuts."

Miss Ketterman said, "I found Connie quite distraught, incoherent and difficult to understand half the time." Ketterman looked at Martha, "I did not see Martha in the Locker room." She gave Martha a quizzical look. Students agreed with the Miss Ketterman, that they did not see Martha there.

Martha mumbled. "I was in a stall in the back."

"In the back?" Miss Ketterman wondered, "I could not understand Connie and I was right in front of her. I don't know how anyone in a stall on the other side of a wall could understand her."

"Never-the-less, Michael did not assault Connie." Elizabeth stressed, glaring at Martha. "If anything, he saved her life."

I thought that was a bit exaggerated but did not say so. However, I said, "A cop, Officer Kane, has been spreading stories. I understand he is Martha's cousin. He is spreading her tales… he is also an old, longtime friend of the McCaskeys. Needless to say, they do not like me very much."

Coach Cord said, "Billy and Jimmie were close friends. They played on the football team. Billy was *suspected* of being part of the gang that attacked Coach Lockhart but not all of the gang was named."

Martin and Trestler had the teachers schedule meetings with classes to explain the truth and to encourage the students to do their part to dispel the rumors. Martin warned that anyone gossiping or spreading the rumors would be subject to discipline.

I wondered to myself how he was going to discipline himself… he was hardly guiltless in my mind. I did not think they would stop the gossip that easily. Mom and Elizabeth agreed.

CHAPTER 16

As we left the library my mother warned, "You know this is not over."

Elizabeth said. "Yes, rumors do not go away easily. Rumors are the spark that starts a fire; stomping out the spark does not put the fire out. No matter what you do there is damage."

We continued to meet people who did not want to believe "nothing happened". They wanted to "teach me a lesson". Often, if someone recognized my truck, they apparently felt compelled to say something. Connie was repeatedly warned about the "vicious fiend" she was keeping company with. The old black truck with extravagant flames painted around the fenders and hood and the chrome exhaust pipes, stood out. I thought about repainting it... bright red perhaps.

Exasperated, Ian and my father came up with an idea. Dad said. "We have to do something to stop this nonsense." I thought oh boy this is going to be good.

Ian said. "We can have a family dinner together... at Tulane's dance club, maybe Saturday evening."

"Yeah." Dad said. "We can show we are one big happy family."

I guess my skeptical look got my mother's attention. She scowled at me and admonished, "Tulane's is a fancy place. You be on your best behavior. This is to show the township we are one big happy family and there is nothing between us. So, you *will* be on your best behavior." I smiled mischievously. "I mean it, Michael."

Liz put her arm around Connie and pulled her close. "That means you too, dear." Connie scowled, knitting her brows and pursing her lips.

My father said. "I will invite Jerry Mahoney to come and take pictures and write a column for the Mechanicsburg Chronicle. I can write something for the paper too." I was thinking, pessimistically, that we were probably throwing gas on the fire. Connie agreed, but it was our parents' idea so we went along; besides it sounded like it could be a fun night.

"I can help with that." Ian smiled. "We'll see if we can give them something else to talk about."

At the dinner Connie and I were getting cozy when Ian nudged me and said loudly, "We are trying to kill rumors here, you two, not start them."

Connie retorted. "Aren't we trying to give them something else to talk about?" Her father scowled.

All evening whenever Connie and I began to dance close our parents broke in on us. The only time we danced uninterrupted was fast dances.

Connie observed cheekily, "I didn't get this much attention all through school."

"I'm getting more practice dancing than in the past eleven years." I added. "The way you are all trying so hard to keep us apart, aren't you sending the wrong message to this crowd?"

"Aren't we trying to show the township that we are *one big happy family?*" Connie asked. That drew glares from all our parents. But they eased up on their interference and late in the evening Connie and I were relaxing, enjoying a slow dance, when we were interrupted again, but not by our parents.

"Young lady, do you know who you are dancing with?" A well-dressed middle aged woman interrupted us.

"Ho boy, here we go", I thought.

"Yes." Connie glanced at me. "This is my boyfriend, Michael."

"That... *boy*... is a monster. He cut up a girl at the high school. You should stay away from him."

"Yes, but he's, *my* monster." She hugged me.

"Does your mother know who you're with? He's a rapist."

"Heaven's, Madam, where do you hear such nonsense? Michael is the perfect gentleman."

"The police have been looking for him for weeks." Her companion snapped. "He is notorious throughout the region for beating people up."

I said in mock surprise. "I keep hearing about 'the police looking for me'... but I have not been hiding." I waved my hands. "I'm here. Where are the police? Who are these people I am supposed to have beaten up?" I looked around the room.

Connie said. "*You* are spreading gossip, Madam. Michael has never attacked anyone."

"Tell that to the girl he slashed you stupid child. *She* will open your eyes!" The woman turned to walk away.

"*Hey! Don't make* stupid *accusations and walk away.*" She lifted her skirt to expose her thighs and the stitches, scratches and scars. A mixture of gasps and laughter filled the dining room. "*I am that girl. He did* NOT *slash me! I fell in a briar patch!"* She swung around. *"Stop spreading gossip, people. There was no attack."* She lowered her skirt. *"You are all worse than children."*

"Connie, for god's sake." Ian held Elizabeth back from coming onto the dance floor.

"What, Mother. We came here tonight to try to lay this nonsense to rest… so let's lay it to rest."

"I agree Mrs. McCormick." I spoke. "It may be a little dramatic, but maybe that's what it will take to get peoples' attention."

"But good heavens, Constance," Ian protested, "Do you have to display yourself for all to see?" He pointed at the photographer who was taking pictures. Connie smiled, smoothed her skirt and stood closer to me, trying to hide behind me.

I shrugged. "She isn't showing any more than she does when she's cheerleading." Connie poked me in the ribs. "In front of huge crowds… of strangers." Connie poked me several times again as she giggled.

We sat down but the restaurant was filled with the babble, and some laughter, as the patrons reflected on the events of the evening. We certainly got them talking, for better or for worse. I wanted to disappear. I had spent far too much time as the center of attraction as far as I was concerned.

We were back at the table for several minutes and Mom looked around and spoke. "Where is Jimmy? I haven't seen him for a while. He should have been back by now."

Ian looked around, "Maybe he's in the restroom."

I saw Mom and Elizabeth exchange looks. A bar was near the restrooms. After a few minutes of reflection, I excused myself and headed for the door.

"Michael, where are you going?" Mom asked.

"To the restroom, I've been scoffing down too many cokes. I'm about to bust."

I came from the restroom and hesitated before turning toward the bar. I found dad sitting with Ian who had joined him. I walked in and sat next to my father; he was facing the other way listening to Ian.

Ian was saying. "Jim, you need to make things right with Anne. This is not going to help." He pointed at Dad's half full glass.

"It helps me forget."

"Do you really want to forget your wife or your family?"

"I want to forget that I beat the crap out of my kid and hit my wife." Jim muttered. "I have always despised bullies and men who abused their children, or their wives, and now I'm one of them. How do you like that for irony? I am a bully and child abuser. That is what I want to forget."

"Jim you are not a bully, or a child abuser. You need to stop…"

"Hi dad. What are you doing?" He swung around on his stool.

"What are you doing here, Michael? You should not be in here."

"Mom is sick. I thought you should know."

"What… uh, Sick? What do you mean…?"

I gave a sickly smile, "I mean she's worried sick about you. You're drinking has her worried. She misses you."

"She doesn't need me, and you shouldn't be here. It's against the law. You should leave."

"I came here to see you. You need to come back and be with Mom… and me." I pointed at the drink. "This will only cause more talk. Mom doesn't need that right now. She needs you."

Jim turned back to his drink. "You don't need me. Your mother doesn't need me. Go away."

"Mom thinks she needs you. You should come back to the table with us."

"Michael, I told you to leave. Leave now!" He spoke loud and harsh. I backed away warily. Ian touched Dad's shoulder. The room became quiet.

"Is this your answer, Dad? Getting drunk… again?" I protested. "Isn't that what started this? Being drunk?" I sneered as I backed away. "I thought you were more of a man than that. God, help me, I don't understand why, but Mom loves you. Between you and Mom I don't know who amazes me more." I walked out before he could answer.

I went back to our table; Dad and Ian followed. The rest of the evening was quiet, and I avoided looking at Dad.

I was relieved when Connie asked me to dance. We left the table for one more dance… a pleasantly uninterrupted dance as it turned out. We became cozy and we kissed. She put her head on my shoulder as we finished the dance and returned to the table. Liz commented to her husband. "Do you think maybe they were dancing too close, dear? I've never seen anyone dance with their lips." Connie rolled her eyes.

CHAPTER 17

Connie and I went tobogganing on the mountain a few days before Christmas. A fresh snowfall created a Currier and Ives like scene over the mountainside and the countryside below. Our neighbors came in horse drawn sleds from the farms, bringing many children and parents. Everyone was bundled up against the cold and the snow covering the hill was busy with laughing, screaming children, and parents.

"Say, have you taken your flight test?" I asked Connie as we prepared to fly down the hill.

"Just the written exam. I take the flight test on the twenty-third… Daddy's Christmas present. All I have to do is pass."

"I'm sure you will."

"Not if I can't control my emotions. After the past weeks I'm having my doubts."

"You'll be alright. Mister Kelly has scheduled me to take the written exam the first week in January." I studied the hill waiting for kids to clear the bottom. "We should do something for Christmas. A dinner or something."

"We have family in for Christmas day and I will be busy most of the week. Maybe we can do something after Christmas, maybe New Year's Eve. Our parents will be celebrating at the legion."

"They have bands playing at the Highwayman and it's far enough away from Valleyview that we should avoid any trouble."

"I would like that. Maybe we can enjoy some peace for once. Let's do that." We sped down the slope, laughing as we crashed into a snow bank.

We arrived at The Highwaymen early on New Year's Eve and found a quiet booth in the back. The Highwaymen was a favorite nightspot east of York, a trucker's haven most of the time, except on weekends. It was popular with locals, and talented youth bands from the region provided entertainment. It was busy because of New Year's Eve, and we hoped that with the crowd we would be unnoticed.

"I'm jealous that you have your license before me." I joked.

"Oh, I'm *so sorry.*" She did not look sorry.

"No, you aren't"

"Your right." She laughed and giggled as I poked her side.

We had a pleasant dinner while crowds in the adjacent bar started New Year's celebrations early. We settled into snuggling in the booth between dances. The festivities became louder and livelier as the evening wore on.

A gang of rowdy young men entered the restaurant from the bar, well into their cups. Truck drivers at the counter groaned and shook their heads. They were looking for a quiet respite from a day on the road.

"Oh no." Connie muttered, "That's Terry. What is *he* doing here? I thought he was still at college. I hope he doesn't make a scene."

Terry Goodman was Connie's abusive ex-boyfriend, and a friend of McCaskeys. My content feeling of moments before was replaced by a troubled quiet feeling.

The young men settled in a booth on the opposite side of the dance floor. Terry did not appear to notice us. I did not expect that to last; especially if we got up to dance.

"Do you want to leave?"

"No. I'm ok. Anyway, I'm tired of being intimidated by him. I never should have gone with him. It was not what I expected. He was overbearing and cruel... abusive... a control freak. I had never been treated like that and I didn't know what to do. I didn't like the feeling of being out of control. *You* be careful. I don't want you to get into trouble because of me."

"Me?" I smiled. "When have I made trouble?" She gave me a look, her mouth twisted suspiciously.

"I know you don't *make* trouble, but you seem to attract it, you and your brothers. You are magnets... especially where the McCaskeys are concerned."

She was probably right, and I became wary when I saw that Terry had noticed us. I caught him staring at us.

We got up to dance and shortly he came to break in. He asked Connie to dance with him. She seemed reluctant but I suppose she did not want trouble and consented to a dance. The dance went ok but when it finished Terry would not let go of her hand and tried to drag her back to his table.

"Terry, stop." She tried to pull free. "Let go! I'm with Michael."

"You're *my* girl. He can find someone else. You're with me now."

She struggled trying to pull her hand loose. *"Terry, let go, you're hurting me!* I am not going with you."

He growled and shook her roughly which got the attention of the truckers. I was out of my seat and crossing the floor as he growled, "We're finished when I say we're finished. You're my girl and no one takes my girl."

"Terry!" I yelled.

Connie looked worried and shook her head at me. "I am *not* you're girl, Terry. I'm tired of you bullying me. It's over, now let go."

The truckers began to stand up. The proprietor looked worried and called for security.

"You *need* to listen to her, Terry. Let go of her." I was halfway across the floor.

Terry's friends started to get up, but several truckers glared at them. One large driver growled in a deep bass.

"You fellas should relax." The gang was not too drunk apparently. They sat down.

"Do you think you can beat me like you did the McCaskeys? Yeah, I heard about that, Hunter. Maybe you need someone to bring you down a peg." Terry tightened his grip on Connie's arm, and she kicked him in the shins. He let go and she backed away.

"I am not with you. We are done. We were done when you went to college. Go away and stop making trouble."

"I'll show you trouble, bitch." He threw a punch at her, but she blocked it. He looked shocked and took another swing. She caught his arm, spun around, ducked under his arm and twisted. I had to jump out of the way as the big athlete flipped head over heels, landed on his back, rolled under a table and hit his head.

I had forgotten that Connie and several of the girls had taken an interest in Kim's martial arts classes. I was impressed and amused.

Her voice sounded a little nervous as she swept her hair back and shook her head. "I think we should leave, Michael." Her eyes and voice betrayed her calm as she picked up her coat and bag and headed for the door. She nodded to the cashier as I paid our bill. "I'm sorry about the mess Sir."

"No problem. We appreciate entertainment... sometimes. We'll have more of this before the evening is over." He watched as Terry struggled to stand up. The tumble, on top of too much booze, was catching up to him. He stumbled around trying to get his bearings. A couple of big men, employees of the facility, watched him and stood back as he appeared about to upchuck. The proprietor told the men to get him out back before he messed up the floor.

"I will have the boys show these guys the door." The proprietor smiled, raised his eyebrows and spoke. "Maybe later, after you two make your exit. We wouldn't want an encore in the parking lot."

The snow had started again while we were in the restaurant and the drive home was slow. She cuddled up next to me.

"Where did you learn that little trick?" As if I didn't know.

"You are not the only one who knows about Kim's martial arts school."

I laughed. "Yeah, he said he was going to start a school in his garage."

"After CC told us about you and Mac's gang… and of course we all know about you and John… we got together and went to see Kim."

I laughed. "It looks like you were doing more than talking."

I tried to put my arm around her, but I had to keep working the gearshift to control the truck in the snow. I drove slowly, taking the long way home up the river road. She was asleep on my shoulder when I parked up the road from her home and shut the engine off.

"We're here."

She opened her eyes. "Michael, my home is down there. Are you going to make me walk home… in the snow?" She kissed me and giggled. "Are you afraid of my father?"

"Who, me?" I put my arm around her, pulled her close and kissed her. She relaxed and I caressed her face gently, kissing her and enjoying her warmth. "I thought maybe I would try to rev up *your* motor."

"Uhum." She purred softly and pressed closer.

We sat holding on to each other for a long time, leaning against the door as I listened to her breathe. I mused that something so simple gave me so much pleasure. We dozed off.

A sharp rap at the window startled me awake. I sat up thinking a car had hit us, but Connie muttered, "Oh no. Daddy's here."

"No, not Daddy." I shaded my eyes as a flashlight beam blinded me. "A cop."

The officer spoke roughly, "Hey, what are you kids doing here?"

I rolled the window down part way. "What? What is it, officer?"

"I asked; what you were doing here?"

"Nothing. Just sitting, talking."

"That didn't look like talking to me. Get out here. Now!" He commanded.

I was annoyed at the intrusion, but I hurried to get out of the truck. Connie had to climb out on my side because of a pile of snow on the other side.

We stood together at the side of the road, holding hands as the young cop studied Connie. "You're Terry's girl, aren't you?"

"No, I'm Ian's girl. Commander Ian McCormick."

"Don't be smart with me girl. I know who you are. You're Connie, Terry Goldman's girl. I know that much."

"I am not *Terry's girl.*" She answered petulantly. I worried that she would anger the cop. Because of his youth I assumed this was officer Kane.

I asked, "What's this about, Kane? You are Billy Kane, aren't you?"

"That is *Officer Kane* to you boy." I thought it was ludicrous for him to call me boy considering he was just a few years older than me. "You shouldn't be parking here, Hunter. I know you... you're a troublemaker. I got a call. You were making trouble at the Highwayman, and I've been watching for you."

"Your information, as usual, is wrong. There was no trouble and anyway that's not in your jurisdiction." I thought, the way I see it you are the one making trouble, but I said, "I don't see why I can't park here. We aren't on the road."

Kane got up in my face. "Cause I say you can't, now move on."

"Michael." Connie cautioned. We got in the truck and drove to her home a short distance down the road and pulled into the driveway. Connie jumped from the truck and as I came around the back a snowball smacked me in the face. She stood there laughing as I brushed the snow off and spit out a few flakes.

"You want to play? Just wait." I ran onto the snow covered yard, scooped up a handful of snow and as she bent to scoop up another handful of snow, my snowball hit her square in the bum.

"Ooh." She howled and charged at me with a handful of snow. She leaped on my back as I bent to make a snowball. We fell together and rolled around screaming and laughing, trying to wash each other's faces with cold white stuff.

A loud shout stopped our play. *"Hey! Just what do you two think you are doing?"*

Kane was stomping toward us across the yard.

"We're playing. What's it look like."

"You were supposed to be taking her home!"

"I am home." Connie put her hands on her hips in disgust. "This is my home you silly duck."

"You be quiet girl. I'm talking to this troublemaker. I don't think Terry's going to be happy with you fooling around with his girl."

"*I told you, I am not Terry's girl.* I don't see what business that is of yours anyway." She yelled at the aggravating cop. "Terry has nothing to say about what I do. He doesn't own me."

I growled, "Kane, you've been making enough trouble for us for weeks. It's time you went and rolled some drunks and stopped bothering us."

Kane pulled his nightstick out. That scared me and I braced myself; I didn't know how I was going to fight a cop without getting into trouble. "I'll bother you, boy." I suspected that was what he wanted, an excuse to arrest me.

"Officer Kane!" Commander McCormick walked quickly from the carport, covering the distance to Kane in four easy strides. "Is there a problem?" Ian glanced at the night stick and glared at the youthful cop.

"These kids are making too much noise, disturbing the neighbors." Kane protested.

McCormick let his eyes wander over the fields around the house. "What neighbors? There are no neighbors within a hundred yards. It is New Year's Eve. Who *isn't* making noise?" We could hear a celebration at a house down the road. "You should be in Etters, watching for drunk drivers. You are the one causing a disturbance and you are trespassing… without a warrant, or cause. I'll thank you to leave."

"Listen McCormick just because you're a Commander…" He backed up hastily as Ian stepped toward him. Ian was very tall, and Kane looked small beside him.

"*Leave! Now!* Get off my property."

Kane huffed and hastily retreated to his car.

Ian turned to us. "You kids are out late, and you are making a lot of noise." He looked at his watch and then at Connie. "Its 12:15 young lady you should be inside. You could get in trouble out here."

She looked indignant, her fists on her hips. "Daddy, I'm not a little girl anymore and as *you* pointed out it is New Year's Eve."

"Yes, I am aware of that, but you have a big day tomorrow, remember? At the old folks home. The special program, remember?" Their church was putting on a special music program at the home for the elderly. "You have to be at the church early. And I know you're not a *little girl* anymore." He glanced at me without smiling. "That's the trouble. I *saw* you stop down the road. So don't think you are putting anything over on me."

She sighed. "A few minutes aren't going to matter."

He leveled a cautionary finger at her and then pointed at me. "A few Minutes." As he turned to walk back to the carport, Connie picked up a handful of snow.

"Connie? No." I muttered warily. She sent the snowball flying. It smacked her father in the middle of the back. He stopped, frozen for a moment in place, and then slowly turned.

Connie pointed at me. "He did it! He did it!"

I jumped, my hands raised. "No—no—no!" Ian glared at me, a wicked grin on his face as he packed a large snowball. "Now-now, Commander."

Connie warned. "Now you're in for it buster. You better run." She let out a surprised yelp as the snowball smacked her. The scene degenerated into a free-for-all, snowballs flying in every direction. Connie protested as we ganged up on her, pelting her with snow.

A snowball sailed in from the house and hit Ian in the back of the head. He turned to see Elizabeth on the veranda, packing another snowball. She was wearing a light house dress. Her second snowball whizzed by my head. I barely ducked in time. She laughed. "Hey sailor-boy, you better stop picking on my daughter."

Ian scooped up a handful of snow and started up the steps. "So! You want to play, little girl?" Elizabeth screamed and fled inside, pursued by her wickedly cackling husband. He shouted over his shoulder, "A few minutes, and then inside, young lady." As he went inside. "Woman, you are in trouble." There was a hilarious scream from inside.

I pulled Connie close and wrapped my arms around her.

"Not here." She grabbed my hand and we fled to the shadows of the carport where we hugged and kissed and held each other.

"When can I see you again? Next week?"

"*Connie!* One minute." Ian called from inside.

She laughed and yelled, "Clock watching spoil sport!" She whispered, "I have to go. Call me next week."

CHAPTER 18

"Take your time, Michael and don't rush." Kelly was going over last minute instructions as I inspected the Cessna. He was making me nervous, as if I were not nervous enough.

"I am ready, don't worry, Mister Kelly, I'll be ok." I wished I could convince myself of that.

Kelly worried like a mother hen when students were ready to take their flight tests. "I know you are, but sometimes the test can be intimidating, and you can draw a blank at critical moments. Do you have all your papers in order? Do you know where to find them?"

"Yes, they're here." I showed him, "and I have the charts for the cross country."

The day seemed to drag on as the inspector, Mister Smith, put me through the mill on aircraft manuals, preflight planning, and emergency procedures.

I planned a 201 mile flight to Erie with a stop at Bradford. According to the FAA manual, the inspector would probably conduct impromptu exercises during the flight such as emergencies or changing my destination and I probably would not go all the way to Erie.

The weather forecast was for all clear to the west. I made a note of a storm on the east coast. I presented my plan to Smith, and he agreed that the storm would not be a problem. Fuel services topped up the fuel and I started the engine, performed checks, and set the radios as the engine warmed up. I took off, climbed to 8500 feet and set course for Bradford.

Twenty minutes into the flight Smith abruptly told me to go to Sunbury. I recalculated my new course, making quick calculations, let ATC know at Harrisburg of my change, and prepared to turn, checking the sky around us for traffic.

"Are we clear?" I asked.

"Clear on the right." He called as he looked back to the right.

I began to bank to the right and cut the power to descend to 7500 feet. I had almost completed the turn when Smith yelled. "Pull up! Pull up! Geese! Damn they came up from below and behind."

I applied full power and pulled back on the wheel. There was a shudder as something struck the plane. I saw geese scattering on every side as white feathers obscured the windshield momentarily before blowing away.

"Snow Geese. They were behind and below us. I couldn't see them. Sorry" Smith said. "We turned right into them. Are we ok?"

I scanned the instrument panel and tested the controls. "Controls seem ok. The impact was hard though… I think some of the geese were above us. I think one or more hit the prop."

"Yeah, lots of feathers. We may have damage. We should look for a nearby airport and check for damage. This is as good a time as any to do an emergency landing exercise." I began checking my charts as I continued my descent. "Snow Geese feed in the fields below but January seems too early for them. I haven't seen them this high before. Usually, Canada Geese are the problem."

I moved the throttle lever. "Uh-oh, I think we took a hit in the engine. The throttle is not responding." The throttle and mixture had no effect. "The rpm is dropping. We are losing power. Beaver Springs was right ahead about nine miles, to the right of our course. Snook is a grass field southwest about six miles."

Smith checked the chart. "We have enough power. Go for Beaver. Hold at seven thousand feet as long as possible and descend when we are clear of the mountains."

"I am declaring an emergency."

Smith watched the instruments as I let Harrisburg know, "We are losing power after a bird strike. We are heading to Beaver Field." The engine soon sputtered and died. "Harrisburg. We have lost power. We are three minutes out of Beaver Airfield, and we are over Bald Eagle Park. I do not see any closer place to land." Harrisburg control acknowledged.

Smith shook his head, "Well we *were* planning an emergency test." He looked at me. "You up to this. Or do you want me to take over?"

"I'm okay. Just don't go far away." He laughed.

I set up a glide slope, hoping we had enough altitude to reach Beaver. "Keep an eye out for a safe place to land though… just in case." We both scanned the terrain below. There was nothing but trees and mountains. Shortly, we had the airport in sight, and I was sure we could reach the runway. Smith raised the field on the radio, declaring an emergency and reported we had no power… it would be a dead stick landing. Beaver Airfield did not have a tower, but they acknowledged and asked if we needed emergency services. Mister Smith told them we should be able to make the runway, but we might come down short.

I aligned with the runway and touched down just over the threshold. We coasted off the runway at the first turn-off.

A check of the engine revealed that at least one goose had been ingested into the cowl and had damaged the throttle controls and there was a developing oil leak.

Smith discussed the event over lunch and reviewed my flight and the emergency.

"I was going to test you on emergency procedures, but you handled the real thing very well."

"That is not the first emergency I've had to deal with. I had a medical emergency last year during a cross country… my instructor collapsed."

"I heard about Carl Anderson."

The plane would have to wait to be repaired. Another plane came up from Harrisburg and we flew back to Harrisburg. I passed my test and got my license. We had a celebration at Harrisburg as I described the adventure to my fellow pilots and my parents.

But I guess I showed too much pride and that was like placing a steak in front of a hungry lioness. My mother was happy for me, but her enthusiasm was dampened by worry about my attitude. She and Dad were pleased that I had passed and at Smith's report of how well I handled the emergency.

Dad and I did not talk much since Thanksgiving and he did not say anything when Mom spoke about God and Jesus. He was always in a sullen mood now, but not angry.

"Gee Mom, I would think you would be happy for me. I'm realizing my dream."

"I *am* proud of you Michael, very proud, but you seem to be so focused on your career and school and worldly things, you are neglecting your spiritual needs."

Mom did not talk about the church much anymore, she seemed disappointed in the church, but she spoke a lot about Jesus. If anything, her faith was even stronger, but I could not understand that.

"I am getting along fine without religion, Mom. I am working in the real world, not the fantasy world of the bible. It is getting a little tiresome hearing you always criticizing me when I do well."

She sighed audibly and put her head in her hands as if in prayer. I was about to speak but she spoke first. "I am sorry Michael. I don't mean to be a nag, but—but—I don't know. It is not a fantasy, Michael. It is more real than the things you can see and touch." She appeared about to tear up.

"I trust the things I can touch, not the things I cannot see or touch. Prayer, miracles, people walking on water or magically healing the sick? It all sounds like fairytales to me." I left the room before she could answer; I did not want to see her cry.

Though I protested my unbelief I always had an uncomfortable gnawing feeling inside and for some reason I could not get that book, *Treasures* out of my mind.

CHAPTER 19

On Valentine's Day, Connie and I enjoyed an early evening dinner at the Gifford's Park lodge overlooking Gifford's Lake. It was a quiet romantic evening with dinner and dancing to a professional orchestra.

"We should go flying together sometime, now that you have your license." Connie said.

"Yeah. We could pool our money and lease an airplane. Maybe fly somewhere for a weekend. Florida. Fort Lauderdale. Spring break." I laughed. "Our parents would go nuts. They were wary of us coming here and it's only a fifteen minute drive."

She laughed but continued, "I'm serious, Michael. I was thinking of something a little closer, maybe less ambitious, like Ocean City for Spring Break." She rolled her eyes, "*That* would definitely drive them nuts, especially Dad." She laughed again. "We could fly to Cape May, near Wildwood. That's where we go in the summer. There are boarding houses right on the beach."

"Sounds like fun."

"It will have to be just a day trip. I am really busy with the science club project for the science fair in March."

"You guys are really being secretive. I don't suppose you can tell me what you are doing."

"Hum, can I trust you?" She squinted suspiciously. "Are you a spy?" She grinned as she looked around warily. "If I tell you I might have to shoot you."

"*Hmmm,* how much can I get for the information?" I whispered.

"We have the use of one of those old barns on Tanner Island. The power company put that bridge in on the south end and they are doing some surveying and testing for the new power plant. I am the Science Club secretary, and I am keeping our records. Very professional, if I do say so… keeping good records counts for points in the competition at the fair. It is an aeronautics project. As an apprentice aircraft mechanic, I think you would find it interesting. Woody is in charge."

"Ooh, Woody the brain? It must be fun working with him."

"He's alright… if you stay out of his way."

When we arrived at Connie's home, her parents were not home from the legion party, and we settled down for a quiet evening. Connie brought out snacks and sodas and we danced to her parents' big band records. We were snuggling and getting into the mood with the music when the front window exploded.

A brick bounced off the stereo and we were sprayed with glass as we dove to the floor shocked out of our minds. We scrambled for the kitchen as we were showered with plaster from a hail of bricks flying through the window and tearing up the walls inside. That barrage finished off the big window and smashed the television. Bricks and rocks bounced off walls and furniture. We heard shouting outside.

"I think that's Terry!" Connie said through tears. "What's he doing?"

"Trying to wreck the house is my guess."

"Hey bitch. How's your new boyfriend doing? Is he hiding under the bed yet?"

Connie grabbed the phone from the wall in the kitchen to call the police and I crawled to the front window to try and see who was outside. More projectiles just missed me.

I yelled. "We are calling the police. You better stop and go away before someone gets hurt." After having a quick look and ducking from more bricks, I said, "There appears to be a gang." A projectile destroyed a lamp near me. Bricks continued to fly through the window. I shrank below the window sill.

"Michael, be careful. Those bricks can kill you." She worried.

I yelled again. "Are you guys crazy, or drunk? The police are coming. You better go away!"

"The police are useless. Go ahead, call them. A lot of good that will do you." Terry yelled, *"I'm going to show you and the bitch that you don't make a fool of me and get away with it."*

A gunshot rang out as the bullet crashed into the wall outside. "Get down! Somebody has a gun! I can't believe this."

Terrified, I huddled in a corner by the front door, as a flurry of shots crashed through the wall and the door; one shook me, passing through the door right in front of me. Connie screamed and covered her head as a bullet shattered the plaster over her head showering her with plaster dust.

"Are you hurt?" I yelled.

"No, stay there, Michael." She shouted at me and then she shouted into the phone, *"They're shooting at us for God's sake! Send help! Hurry!"* Her black hair was turning white with plaster dust as more shots tore up the wall.

Someone outside cursed. *"Terry, what the hell are you doing? You didn't say anything about guns."*

"Shut up and throw those bottles. Don't be such a wimp. I'm just trying to scare them." Gunfire shattered another lamp. Terry chortled as he fired wildly into the house. *"Mac should be here. He would love this."* More bricks and rocks came through the window.

"Mac again." I muttered, "Why can't I be rid of him?"

"Why don't the police arrest him?" Connie said as a fire bomb crashed against the veranda. Flames scattered on the snow and quickly extinguished. She screamed. *"What was that?* Oh my God they're going to burn the house down!"

I moaned half serious, "If I had a gun they would change their tune."

Connie exclaimed. "Yes! Of course... Daddy has guns." She crawled on the floor into the hallway and rushed into her parents' bedroom. "The keys are here somewhere." She rushed downstairs to the basement and shortly came back with a Remington pump action and a double barrel shotgun. "Can you use this?" She handed me the double barrel shotgun, after crawling across the living room floor with debris falling around her. She dumped a carton of 12-gauge shells on the floor as she huddled in the corner with me. She began to stuff shotgun shells into the magazine of the pump action while I crawled across to the far corner, wincing with every brick, shot and rock that careened off the sill.

"Michael, for God's sake stay down. Why can't you stay put?"

I was second guessing my move in my mind, but I answered, "I think I can get a better shot from here. You stay there." Bullets pummeled the walls ferociously. I hoped in vain, they would run out of ammo soon. I peeked over the sill. "We should see if we can scare them off. I've never shot *at* anyone. They emphasize *not* doing that during training."

"Yeah, neither have I. I don't want to shoot anyone, but if these don't scare them... then I don't know what will. But I am not going to let them burn my house down." She was fumbling trying to get cartridges into the magazine. Another shot and a bullet whined past close over my head. That got my heart beating faster.

I hastily pointed the shotgun out the window and pulled the triggers. The gun roared and I went flying backward to the floor. My shoulder hurt but I heard panicked shouts outside.

Someone sounded scared. *"Hey. I didn't expect to be in a gunfight. That wasn't in the deal! Let's get out of here!"*

Terry shouted. *"You bunch of cowards! Throw the bombs! They can't see anything. I'll keep them down."* He fired wildly again, bullets hitting all over, most of them hit near me. *"Burn them out!"*

Connie nervously laughed in spite of her tears. She was as scared as me. She finally got the last cartridge in her gun as she mumbled, "Silly rabbit... don't pull both triggers at the same time. I thought you used a shotgun before." She was kneeling and looking out over the windowsill keeping low.

"Yeah, I was in a hurry and forgot about the kick." I rubbed my shoulder. "My shotgun doesn't have two triggers. Do you know how to use that thing?" I reloaded trying to ignore the pain in my shoulder.

"Just watch me smarty." As she peeked over the windowsill. *"Agh, firebomb!"* She hastily raised the shotgun to her shoulder and fired. The kick knocked her back on her bum as a fire bomb burst close to the house. She scowled at me as I laughed nervously.

"What was that?" I laughed, nervous and scared.

"That was too close." She said, "but I got it."

"I think some of that got on the roof." I squinted over the edge of the window. "There are four guys I think."

Connie pumped the gun and fired again, while sitting on the floor this time. She fired over the windowsill and a firebomb shattered short of the house. She had to scurry back into the corner as a flurry of shots struck the window's edge near her.

"Good shot." I said as I looked for a target. "I think I can see a carton near the car. I wonder," I tried to steady my nerves and aim, "if I can hit that…" I braced and fired, twice, and was rewarded with a bright plume of flames lighting the night. A small tree caught fire lighting the front yard. That drew curses and shouts from our tormentors. "I think their car is on fire." I snuck a peek over the sill.

Terry shouted and threw another bottle vowing to burn us out. He was lit up by the flames, an easy target and Connie shattered the bottle as he released it. The flaming gas flew back at him. He screamed. *"I'm on fire. Oh shit, I'm burning. The bitch has burned me."*

"What's the matter, Terry? Don't like your own medicine?" Connie screamed. And then muttered, "Oh God, I hope I didn't hurt him. I don't want to hurt him… too much."

Someone yelled, *"Terry, get in or we're leaving without you."*

We fired at the car as it backed down the driveway and saw a headlight got dim. As they turned and roared away, we fired parting shots. "I think we hit a taillight." She spoke.

"Yeah… and I think I hear a siren."

"Finally."

The carton continued to explode as flames reached other bottles. A siren from up the road was answered by another one from the direction of York Landing.

"That was quick." I spoke. "I thought the police would be thirty minutes away."

"Maybe it's from the fire house in York Landing."

"One is coming from Yokumtown. I hope it is not Kane… he hangs around Etters at the Farm. We better watch our step. Your Dad isn't here now. You better put the guns away."

"Why? We didn't do anything wrong. They attacked us. Look… the house is wrecked." She surveyed the room with a pained expression. A shelf full of memorabilia was wrecked as well as the TV, most of the lamps and many pictures on the walls. Plaster was all over the furniture and carpet.

"Kane will not care about that. He'll twist it around."

"He'll be looking for an excuse to hassle you, Michael."

"Your father didn't ingratiate himself on New Year's Eve. Kane will be looking for a way to get back at both of us… we are on our own." She took the guns back to the basement.

She came back as a cop car hit a patch of snow and ice, slid past the drive onto a pile of snow beside the driveway. We were not surprised when Kane jumped out, yelling and screaming incoherently. He came slipping and sliding up the driveway, waving his gun and yelling obscenities.

Connie and I nervously sat on the couch holding each other and trying to look innocent as Kane stormed onto the veranda and glared in through the shattered window. "All right you two what's going on here? Get your hands up right now both of you. Drop your guns."

"We don't have guns." Connie said as Kane climbed in through the shattered window opening. We held our hands in the air as Kane waved his pistol at us. I was afraid he would shoot us by accident.

"Don't give me no crap I heard gunfire. Where are the guns?"

"A bunch of guys outside had guns. They shot up the house and tried to burn it." Connie pointed at the living room wall pocked with bullet holes. "They almost killed us."

"They were throwing bricks and firebombs." I spoke. "They took off before you came. You just missed them. You probably passed them on the road."

He stuffed the pistol back into his holster after several clumsy attempts. "Don't give me that crap. It looks to me like you were having a party here. When the folks are away, the kids will play. You're under arrest."

"For what?" Connie protested. "Look around. You can see someone was throwing stuff from outside. There was no party. You're crazy."

"Yeah, look at the bullet holes in the walls. Come on Kane." I prompted.

"That's Officer Kane to you, punk." He sneered as a fire truck pulled into the driveway. Firefighters quickly doused the tree fire and doused the remnants of fire in front and under the carport. "Don't give me any lip. You're both under arrest. We'll see how smart your old man is now."

The fire chief, in a white helmet, looked at the scorched façade. "What's going on here, Kane? You got here quick." Chief Wilson looked in through the broken window, took in the mess in the living room and asked us. "What happened? It looks like someone's been throwing bricks and fire bombs."

I spoke. "Yeah, some guys were out front. Their bottles blew up and set the tree…"

"Shut up, Hunter. He was talking to me."

"Were you here, Kane?" Wilson asked. "I was talking to them. I'm sure I saw you pull up just ahead of us." He glanced over his shoulder at the cop car sitting on the pile of snow. "Yeah. I can see you're on top of it."

"Don't be a smart ass, Wilson. Just do your job and put the fire out. I'll take care of the cop business."

"If it involves a fire, it *is* my business." He glanced at the wall outside and the living room wall. "Someone appears to have been shooting at the house. That would be your business."

"Yeah, and I've got the troublemakers right here."

I retorted, "That's crap, Kane. You were sitting up the road and called your buddy Terry when we came home. That's the only way he could have known we were here. You waited up the road waiting for your buddy to finish trashing the house. You are both doing Mac's dirty work."

"Yeah, how else could you hear gunfire if you were not close by?" Connie asked.

Kane knocked me back down on the couch and appeared ready to cuff Connie. "You watch your mouth." Kane roughly fastened the handcuffs on my wrist and Connie's. "Like I said, you're under arrest, and so is your girlfriend." Connie winced and protested at the tightness of the cuffs and Kane raised a hand as if to strike.

"Hey, Kane. Watch the rough stuff. You're be'in awful rough, aren't you?" A firefighter protested. "They're just kids."

"Mind your own business."

"I am." The fireman replied.

Kane scowled at him. I looked at Connie and said in a hoarse whisper. "He's predictable."

She answered, "Yes, but it would be better if we didn't provoke him." She grimaced. I grinned and shrugged.

"Hey, I told you two to shut up."

We projected innocent expressions and shook our heads. He hauled us out to his car. We stood in the cold, with no coats, while he got help from the firemen to get his car off the pile of frozen snow. He hauled us off to the jail, leaving the firemen to guard the house.

At the police station, he pushed us into a cell together and closed the door.

"Hey, what are you doing? Aren't you gonna take the cuffs off?" I protested and looked around. "You can't put us both in one cell."

"Don't tell me what I can't do in *my* jail."

Connie looked at the tiny cell with just a toilet and a small sink and two narrow bunks. "Hey what if one of us has to go to the bathroom? There's no privacy here."

"Hey girly, now that's your problem isn't it. Maybe I'll just come and watch." He laughed crudely and turned to leave.

I objected loudly, "Hey, come on Kane stop the nonsense. You know you're going to get in trouble if you do this. You could lose your job. There are rules you know. I may be just a kid, but I know this isn't right."

Connie said, "Yeah when my father finds out you're going to be in big trouble."

Kane came back abruptly. We jumped back as he banged on the door with a night stick. "Listen girly, your old man may be a big honcho on that base, but his uniform and all those medals don't mean crap here. This is my jail. I run things here. You service brats are all just a little full of yourselves."

Connie asked, "Aren't you going to look for the guys who wrecked my parents' house? They're getting away."

"I didn't see no other guys. You're making that up to save your own miserable butts. I didn't see anyone else." He headed for the door, "I ain't gonna stand here listening to your whining. Make yourselves comfortable." He laughed viciously. "I'm sure you can think of ways to entertain yourselves." He slammed the door.

We settled onto a bunk and after some trial and error, found a comfortable position and fell asleep. We were exhausted after the chaotic evening.

I heard Ian shout. Connie was still asleep and did not stir at her father's voice. I peeked. Ian was looking through the bars. He turned to Kane. "What the hell is this Kane? You put a couple of kids… a boy and a girl in the same cell."

"We don't have much in the way of accommodations here Commander." Kane grinned. "Besides I doubt it would be the first time they spent the night together."

Ian balled his fist and looked like he was about to pounce. Kane appeared scared as he stepped back. Elizabeth pushed past, giving her husband a warning look. "Open this, officer, please."

He warily squeezed past the commander and opened the cell door. She looked at the empty bunk and the two of us in the one bunk. Pretending to be asleep I grimaced when she muttered, "They didn't *have* to use one bunk, did they?" She pulled the blanket off and called out, "Ok you two love birds wake…" She grabbed the cufflinks. "What the… *what is this, Officer Kane?"* She lifted the handcuffs.

Connie woke up. "Mother. You're here."

"What time is it?" I asked innocently.

I was shocked when Elizabeth swore. *"You son-of-a-bitch."* Ian stared at his wife, as if he did not know her. We all stared at her. She was never known to be vulgar. *"You left them handcuffed… a boy and girl… together… in the same cell."* I guess there are exceptions. She stepped toward the officer who, suddenly aware of his peril, stepped back and bumped into Ian.

Ian growled in his face, "Can I hit him now, dear?" He had his fist balled, eager to thump the arrogant cop. Kane looked scared now, giving me some little satisfaction.

"I wouldn't if I were you, Ian." Don Klienfeldt entered the cellblock, followed by my mother and father. "I think it would be best if you let the law take care of this." He stared at Officer Kane. "The *officer* here," Klienfeldt spoke authoritatively, "has exceeded his authority. He is in big trouble. I suggest, very strongly, that you take those off the children, right now *Mister Kane.*"

Klienfeldt was a lawyer I had seen at the legion and at the house occasionally. He was a short balding man in his late forties with Truman style, wire rim glasses and wearing a yarmulke. He was dressed in the rumpled trappings of a suit. He wore an equally rumpled white shirt. He had obviously been roused from bed, and he had not taken much time to dress. The belligerent cop did not intimidate the lawyer. Klienfeldt looked him in the eye with a confident smile on his face.

Kane griped, "Don't tell me what my authority is, Klienfeldt. This is my jail and I'll run it any way I see fit."

"He keeps saying that." I murmured. Connie stuck an elbow in my ribs, quietly clearing her throat.

Our parents glared at me. Klienfeldt answered, "Oh, he may think that but, he is sadly mistaken. He is going to find out it is not *his* jail, and he cannot run it as *he sees fit*. This is a society of law, not some banana republic. There are rules and he is subject to them." He produced a paper and waved it under the cop's nose. "This is what is called a writ of habeas corpus. You do know what that is, don't you? Release them at once."

The police chief, Richard King, arrived and took in the scene and growled. "Kane! What the hell do you think you are doing? Get those kids out of there. Now."

Dad looked at Ian who appeared puzzled. "When Chief Wilson called and explained what happened I thought it best to call in the big guns." He nodded toward the little lawyer who grinned.

The chief took the paper as Kane removed the cuffs. "You've been a little too free around here Kane. From now on you will be working in the office until further notice."

"I didn't join the police to work in no office."

"You will work where I tell you to."

Klienfeldt announced. "Justice Clark has ordered the children be released into their parent's custody immediately."

Billy Kane was suspended pending a state police investigation. We explained the evening's events to the sheriff, and he called the state police for help. Terry and his friends were caught in Lancaster when he went to a hospital to treat his burns.

Connie and I were the center of local discussion, again. Rather than knocking down the old rumors we had simply changed their focus. Now we were trouble prone lovers.

It was becoming more than a little annoying. I was becoming weary of the limelight. I was eager for the school year to end so I could join the navy and get away from this place. But it was going to be a long time till summer and school's end.

CHAPTER 20

"Michael, could you help me take some cartons over to Tanner Island?" Barry Millar approached me at school.

"Isn't that where you guys are working on the Science project?"

"It is not a very well kept secret." He laughed. "I think the secrecy is silly. But Woody is paranoid." He laughed again. "I suppose that comes from having a parent in the service."

"I could help you, but I am not a member of the Science Club."

Barry waved his hand dismissively. "Don't worry about that. I have the loan of a pontoon boat down at River Park and I don't have anyone to drive it. I am no good with boats and I know you are.

"Say, maybe you can help when we take the project to the Science Fair. If you don't mind us using your truck."

"I will be happy to help, anyway I can." I chuckled, "but, just remember last year when the girls were trying to get me more involved in the class; that got us in all kinds of trouble. You might want to reconsider that request."

He laughed. "Between the debacle last year and that incident on Valentine's Day I don't think you and Connie have a private life anymore. I'm surprised that you don't have a news reporter following you around all the time."

"Yeah, for the gossip column… especially after Connie's demonstration at Tulane's." We both laughed. That story made the newspapers complete with pictures and it was the talk of the district for a long time… until the 'Valentine's Day' massacre.

Dennis and Connie greeted us as we drove the pontoon boat up on a beach at the island. Connie was wearing a pair of oversized coveralls with dirt on the knees and backside. I noticed a screwdriver sticking out of her pocket. Looking her over, I laughed, "You look cute in that. I thought you were just a clerk on this project. Is this the new style for secretaries?"

"These intellectual types are no good with screwdrivers, so they need help from the girls."

Barry grinned. "Hey, there are those who think... and those who do." We saw Woody come out of the barn and Barry added. "And then there are some who *think* they do."

I deadpanned, looking at Dennis. "You don't actually let her use tools, do you?" Nodding my head toward Connie.

Dennis's amused look over my shoulder warned me that Connie was close. I heard her murmur. "I know how to use a shotgun, too."

Dennis laughed, "You better watch yourself lover boy."

"Lover boy?" Connie and I intoned together.

Dennis raised his hands. "I didn't mean anything. I mean it's no secret you two are going together. The rumor is that you are going to burn the town down next." He smiled and hunched his shoulders as if he expected to be hit.

"Careful Dennis. Now *you* are taking your life in your hands." Connie muttered, "I'm getting a little tired of the home wrecker jokes, boys." She joked. "I *do* know how to use a gun... and I know where you live. A little bird shot solves many annoyances."

Barry and Connie showed me around the science project, a wind tunnel to show the effects of speed on aircraft.

I saw a familiar shape covered with a tarp at the back of the barn. Its telltale shape drew my attention. It was a disassembled airplane. I asked about it and was amused when they became wary and evasive.

I mused aloud, "It looks like one of those old airplanes people leave in old barns when the owner stops flying or dies. The relatives don't know what to do with them. Some guys at Gifford's Point rebuilt a Piper Cub and a Taylorcraft they found in barns, last year."

"You've got your license now, don't you?" David Allen said. "That's quite an achievement."

"Why? Are you thinking of rebuilding it for yourself?" Woody sounded annoyed.

"That's an interesting thought. I've spent my life building models... and I built that boat last year. The thought of building a real airplane is tempting; but I don't have the money... or the time... I'm way too busy now."

"What kind of work are *you* doing that could be so important?" Woody asked

"Kim took me on as an apprentice aviation mechanic last year at Harrisburg, and I am working for Doug Crombie in the electronics shop from time to time.

"Are you guys planning to do something with this? I would think it would be a good project for the science club... or the pilot's club."

David stammered, "Uh, no not at all."

"None of us are pilots." Woody added.

"I am." Connie responded.

"Oh yeah, well I meant none of the boys." Woody replied tartly. I studied him doubtfully.

"Yeah." David corrected, "None of us are pilots *yet*. Dennis and I are close to soloing."

"I soloed last December." Dennis corrected.

"In December?" I was surprised. "Congratulations."

Dennis and I had not spent much time together this year. His father had an issue with me over my *socialist* racial views and he thought the debacle at thanksgiving was proof of my corruption in his eyes. Also, Dennis had started working part time at the New Cumberland Army Depot and he left school early and he worked many weekends.

"Hey congrats, Dennis. That's great." David said.

"Do you have something against women pilots, Woody?" Connie asked. "Not that I would fly anything you built."

"Women can't fly airplanes. They are too small and weak; and too emotional… and I don't think they are smart enough."

"What!" Several of the kids spoke at the same time.

Connie snarled, "Ever hear of Amelia Earhart."

"Or the WASPs." I added.

"She crashed and who were the WASPS?" He sneered. "A bunch of insects?"

Connie rolled her eyes and clenched her fists, ready to punch Woody. "She made many record flights."

I laughed. "For all your smarts, you never were much for history, were you? During the war women test flew fighters and bombers… that women built, incidentally."

Connie added, "Yeah, the story was, the men were afraid to fly the B-29. It had a bad rep for catching fire and Colonel Tibbets had two women fly one for them."

"It doesn't really matter does it?" David intervened. He cleared his throat nervously. "We are not planning to build an airplane, are we?" He muttered. Then he shrugged. "None of us have any more time or money than you, Michael."

However, in spite of Woody's obsession with security it was the talk of every grade of high school that the club was working on some kind of 'wind machine'… or an airplane. That made me smile because it seemed to cause discomfort for one club member.

CHAPTER 21

Carol Foster asked, "Hey, what are you guys doing for the prom?" She dropped into a chair after placing sodas on the table. The students were gathered in the student lounge at the close of the science fair. We were celebrating our senior class taking second prize. The fair was winding down, the crowd was dwindling, and participants were heading home. The subject at our table turned to the next big event on the school calendar.

Eleanor said. "We should rent a limousine together for the prom. That way there will be no pre-dance accidents."

Carol mumbled around the straw. "Yeah, no running through the briar patch." She concentrated on taking a sip of her drink while everyone moaned, and I caught Connie's furtive glance.

She rolled her eyes and spoke. "That would be good."

Kathy said. "We could spend the weekend together… maybe have a swimming party and picnic."

Connie asked, "Where? Gifford's Point?"

Eleanor said, "Why don't we go to Wildwood?" Connie looked at me and grinned. "There will be tons of kids there. We could have a blast. Mom and Dad rented a house on the beach during the summer. It should not cost that much for a weekend, for a gang of us."

Connie said, "Yeah, my folks rent a place at Cape May… right on the beach. Michael, Eleanor and I have our licenses. We should fly down."

"That would be too expensive." Dennis muttered. "I mean I like it, but…"

Carol said. "Wow, yeah. But it's a great idea. It would be nice for the gang of us to spend the weekend together. Wildwood sounds great."

I spoke. "I like the idea of Wildwood. I've heard of it, but I've never been there. I flew a cross-country flight to Ocean City… it was about two hours one way. Cape May would be easy."

"Michael and I talked about flying somewhere after he got his license." Connie said.

I spoke. "How many planes are we talking about? It could be expensive."

"Two planes… and a limousine?" Eleanor moaned. "Talk about dreamers." She gave me a glance. "But maybe we can put together enough money between us. And see what we have in a couple of weeks."

I said, "It will cost twenty dollars an hour for each plane. A Cessna or a Piper can make the flight down in one hour." I shrugged. "What? About one hundred dollars? Maybe six or eight of us could swing it. It may be worth a try."

Chuck said. "Well, everyone here has good jobs. It should not be that hard to scratch together a fund. Ten or fifteen dollars a week from eight of us?" Several of the kids did calculations on napkins or the table. "We could probably collect a thousand by May."

"Ten or fifteen a week? Now who's dreaming?" I spoke. But in the back of my mind, I thought *maybe* we could do it… I was not the only dreamer it seemed.

Eleanor said, "That is optimistic, but I think it is worth the effort… at least we could get the limo."

"And even if we have to drive to Wildwood, it would be fun." Carol said.

Connie said, "We can save up our money and see what we have by the middle of May. A weekend get together sounds great."

"Yeah. If we dip into our savings, we could probably swing it," Eleanor said. "If we each contribute."

"I've been saving for college, but I think I can swing that." Chuck said. Dennis looked uncomfortable. He gave me a look and shrugged. I could not tell if he was in or not. He did not say anything.

It was an ambitious plan, but we appointed Connie as our treasurer and pooled our resources for the next two months.

Dennis confided later at school that he would have to sneak a few bucks from each paycheck because his father kept a close watch on him. His father was suspicious of the things he heard were going on at the school. Dennis did not enlarge on that. I thought it might be because of the progressive views of many of our students.

On prom night in May, the limousine picked me up, followed by Dennis, Chuck and Peter. We made the rounds picking up the girls. The prom was a Hollywood Evening complete with red carpet, dozens of parents with cameras and a couple of reporters from local newspapers.

After the merriments we skipped the after prom activities at the legion home, planning to start out early in the morning. I told Mom and Dad that I was going to spend the weekend at Wildwood with Chuck and Pete. Dennis told his father he was going to spend the weekend with the Science club at Gifford's Park.

The girls gave their parents a similar story about a girls' weekend at the shore. We found out later that no one really bought that, especially the girls' fathers. Most of our mothers were close friends and they put two and two together… or maybe four and four.

Early Saturday morning I checked out a Cessna at Gifford's Airpark and the guys and I left Gifford's at eight o'clock. The flight to Cape May took an uneventful hour and we were on the ground and tied down before nine-thirty. Dennis went to arrange for a carryall. Eleanor and the girls landed just as Dennis returned with a souped up `29 Ford Woody Station wagon.

"Hey Ely, what took you so long?" Chuck asked.

"What do you mean? We are on time. You are early. You didn't take any shortcuts with your planning did you, Michael?" Connie asked.

"Me? Shortcuts? No way."

"How long have you guys been here?" Carol asked.

"About ten minutes."

Eleanor said, "Oh, that's right you guys came from Gifford's, that dinky little airport with no traffic. We came from a real airport with lots of traffic."

"Harrisburg has traffic? Who knew?" Dennis asked, and before anyone could continue the insults, he added, "Let's get this show on the road, the meter is running and I'm hungry."

"Already? It's not even noon yet." Eleanor chided.

"Dennis is always hungry." I remarked as we loaded our bags into the Chevy suburban.

Eleanor looked over Dennis's thin frame and muttered loudly. "He *does* need some meat on them bones."

We found the two and a half story house on the south side of town. It had huge wrap-around verandas on both levels and faced the ocean with a beautiful beach stretching for miles.

We were ready to feast and swim. We tossed our bags in our rooms and gathered on the veranda at the back for a barbeque.

A boardwalk stretched from the veranda across the dunes to the beach. The white sand stretched from Sewell Point and the Coast Guard academy to Cape May Lighthouse which was a short walk from the house. An old WWII bunker was down the beach.

After the meal, we all took a bus to Wildwood. A variety of bands, trying to imitate Bill Haley, entertained hordes of young people. The beach was overrun with students from college and high school celebrating the end of the school year.

We avoided the rowdier college gatherings as there was too much booze flowing. We danced to the bands and partied on the beach until evening.

Eleanor came running from the boardwalk. "Guys! Guys! I just saw my father on the boardwalk. I think your father was with him Connie… and yours Kathy."

"Oh No! What are *they* doing here?" Connie said.

"Looking for you I'll bet." I spoke. "What else?"

"Was your mother with him, Ely?" Connie said.

"No. They seemed to be alone, just four of them. I think one of them was Michael's father."

"We should grab a taxi and head back… before they see us." Kathy said.

We went back to the beach house and continued to party, dancing on the veranda and playing on the beach.

Eleanor relaxed with Dennis on the veranda, while Pete and Kathy played at the water's edge.

"Where are Carol and Chuck, Ely?" Connie asked.

"They went down the beach. I lost sight of them about ten minutes ago." Eleanor said.

Connie and I headed out for a walk. We strolled hand in hand down the long wooden boardwalk to the beach and headed south. We enjoyed the warmth of the night and the glow of the moon on the water. We were near the old bunker when we heard someone laughing inside.

We turned around and walked back up the beach a short distance and dropped our towels above the surf line. Connie took her shorts and shirt off to reveal a two piece bathing suit. Hand in hand we ran into the water and frolicked and swam in the moonlight. She tried to get me to swim, making me chase her, but I was not a good swimmer and could not keep up. We played in the surf for a while splashing each other and snuggling. We rested, lying in the shallow water, cuddling and kissing.

I whispered in Connie's ear. "Have you ever gone skinny dipping, Connie?"

"No." She giggled and looked up and down the beach. There was no one in sight as far as we could see. "Someone will see us."

"There's no one around. We are alone. It's so dark no one can see anything anyway."

"The full moon gives a lot of light. I can see you well enough."

"Yeah, but we are close together."

"Have *you* ever gone skinny dipping?"

"Well," I cleared my throat, "Not really. I've never been much of a swimmer…"

"I noticed."

"…and I try to avoid too much sun in the daytime. I burn badly. But it is night now and it's dark."

"I don't know… you go first."

"Me?" I sat up. "Ok." I stood up and grabbed my waist band and hesitated. Then I walked into the water up to my waist. After a moment, I waved my liberated trunks and tossed them at Connie. She giggled as she caught them, stood up and made as if to walk away. "Hey! Where you going?"

She laughed and twirled the trunks over her head. I started out of the water. She backed down the beach as I ran out of the water. Laughing, she ran into the water with my trunks. I followed her into the water but as I came near, she tossed my trunks up onto the beach and swam a few quick strokes, into deeper water.

"Hey! No fair."

Connie stood in chest deep water and as I hesitated, she produced her top and tossed it onto the beach. It landed just above the surf.

I laughed. "What are you going to do if the waves wash that away?"

She tossed the bottom further up the beach. "I have a spare in my bag."

I moved toward her, and she moved farther out and when I started to follow, she cautioned. "Be careful, Michael, this is deep water."

I dropped out of sight, splashing frantically. "Michael!" She came to me quickly, but before she could rescue me, I wrapped my arms around her, stood up and pulled her close. Our bare flesh touching made me warm in spite of the cool water. Cautiously, we held each other, but we were not comfortable with the touch of flesh against flesh, and we separated. We soon relaxed and splashed around and played before settling down and relaxing in the surf on the beach.

She was lying on her stomach in the surf letting the waves roll over her. I was lying next to her, and I touched her shoulder and ran my fingers lightly down her back enjoying the soft warmth of her skin. As I traced her spine she made a slight shiver. I touched her bare bum and gently caressed her leg. She stiffened and she murmured "Please… don't."

I stopped.

"Are you OK?"

She rolled over and sat up, pulling her knees up, and clutching them close to her.

"I don't know. What are we doing, Michael?"

"What do you want to do?"

"I—I can't… I don't think we should, uh, do this."

"Do what?"

"Michael, please don't be coy. Don't tell me you aren't thinking about, uh…"

"About having, uh… *ahem*. Making love. Yeah. I guess."

She took a breath, "I can't do it, Michael. I'm sorry. I'm just not ready."

I kissed her. "That's ok. To tell the truth, I'm not sure I am ready either."

I got up and spoke. "Wait here." I walked up to the beach. A scream came from up the beach, from the bunker.

Connie called out. "Did you hear that?"

"Yeah. Maybe we should go see if someone needs help."

The sound came again, and she cleared her throat. "Uh, I don't think they want help." We heard laughter.

"Oh. Uh, no. I suppose not."

I collected our clothes and brought her swim suit to her. She washed the sand out in the surf.

I stooped to wash the sand from my suit and muttered. "We need to watch out for crabs. I hope no crabs crawled into them while we were swimming. That would be an unpleasant surprise."

Connie tied her top on. I was poised on one foot, ankle deep in the surf, trying to find the leg hole in the dark when she snuck up behind me. "Are you trying to say I have crabs?" She pushed me as I teetered on one foot.

"Aieee!" I fell into the water sputtering from a mouth full of water and trying not to laugh at the same time. I came up coughing up salt water. "You little sneak!" I yelled. She grabbed her towel and ran past me laughing loudly. *"Just you wait."* I pulled my trunks on and stumbled out of the water as she squealed and raced off up the beach.

"Don't forget your towel and shorts, Michael."

As we came up on the veranda Eleanor called "Hi Connie, everything ok? I heard you scream."

"Yeah. Good. Got anything to eat here?"

"No. not really." Eleanor said as she twisted her mouth in a sarcastic expression while looking at the stack of chips and pretzels on the picnic table.

Dennis laughed. "Wow! You went blind. What were you and Michael doing?" He gave me a suspicious look.

"Nothing." We both answered, and Connie threw a wadded napkin at me and hit me between the eyes. She said, "I can see fine." and giggled.

"Did you see Carol and Chuck in your travels?"

Connie rolled her eyes as I replied. "See? More like *heard* them. The bunker." Connie and I flopped into deck chairs.

Eleanor raised her eyebrows. "Oh… nuff said." We relaxed in the beach chairs enjoying the warm breeze off the ocean.

CHAPTER 22

Early Sunday morning the girls wanted to go to church. Dennis and I were not enthusiastic about that, but we gave in to coaxing from the girls. We were about to enter a church when a woman loitering about in front, looked at us and lifted her nose as if sniffing something. She pointed at Pete and Kathy and sneered, "We don't allow their kind here."

"What kind is that, Madam?" I spoke. I thought, here we go again! Hypocrites. Can't get away from them. Why am I not surprised?

"I thought church was for everybody." Eleanor said. Kathy looked like she wanted to say something but kept quiet. I remembered our discussion at summer school.

"Yeah," Connie added, "Jesus said, come onto me *all* you who are burdened."

The woman huffed and retorted, "I don't care what Jesus said. Those people have their own church. Let them go there."

"We are all together." I said and remembered my mother's reply. "My mother would say that Jesus is not here."

Eleanor observed sarcastically, "You don't care what Jesus said? Why do you go to church? We were looking for a place where they worship God… and care what Jesus says." Eleanor turned and huffed, "I don't think we will find him here, Guys… come on, let's go somewhere else." She turned and walked away.

I held Connie's hand as we walked away. "Wow, Ely, I don't think I've ever seen you angry."

Eleanor's face colored as she growled through gritted teeth, "That just makes me so angry. When are people going to grow up?"

I looked at Kathy and we shared a smile. "I wonder what that lady would think if she saw me kissing you"

She colored and Pete said playfully. "I heard about that, flyboy. You better worry about what I would think about that." Everyone laughed. That lightened the mood a little, until we got to the next church.

We found another church a couple of blocks away and we were sitting quietly in a pew, when an usher came and told Pete and Kathy they would have to leave. Everyone was miffed and I was about to say something crude, but Connie grabbed my arm, squeezed tight, and shook her head. Eleanor and Kathy also gave me worried looks and so I clamped my jaws together and fumed inside. We all got up and left.

Eleanor looked as if she was going to cry. She started to apologize to Kathy and Pete, but Kathy hugged her tightly. "It's not your fault."

I spoke caustically, "My dad doesn't go to church. He says they are all just hypocrites and I agree."

"Not *all* churches are like that, Michael!" Connie protested as the others nodded agreement.

"You could have fooled me. The evidence speaks for itself. We're two for two."

"*These* are not *all* churches, Michael." She protested. "There is that Presbyterian mission on the Boardwalk. Everyone is welcomed there."

"You want to go all the way to Wildwood?"

"No!" Eleanor said, "Our fathers may still be there."

"I am sure we can find a good church here." Carol said.

"Yeah, sure." I grumbled.

As we walked back toward the beach house, Pete and Kathy lagged behind. A couple of young teenage black girls came up the road all dressed up.

"Hi, girls." Pete called, "Where you going?"

"We're going to our church over on Canal Road." The older girl replied. "It's the AME church. Come with us. Everyone is welcome."

"We've been looking for a church where we could all go." Pete pointed to the rest of us.

"Come and go with us!" The younger one invited eagerly.

"The churches up the road would not let us all come in." Eleanor said, "We want to all be together. Are you sure your pastor or your parents won't mind having *all* of us come?"

"Oh, for sure. Everyone is welcome at our church. Come on."

I was still skeptical, but the girls led the way and we followed. They took hold of our arms and pulled us along with them. "We're a little late but you *all* will be more than welcome."

A group of smiling parishioners met us in the front yard and enthusiastically invited us in.

I confronted the pastor as we walked up the steps. "You don't mind having a bunch of white kids intruding on your service?" From the look on her face, Connie was not pleased with me.

"It is not an intrusion, young man. This is God's House, and all are welcome in *God's* House. Our precious Lord said, 'come onto me *all* who are heavy laden, and I will give you rest'."

"Yeah, I've heard that, but we were not all welcome in other churches in town. Why should you be any different?"

"Ah, but Our Lord said, 'Do onto others as you would have them do onto you'. If we want others to respect us, we ought to respect them."

"Yeah, but they don't."

He shook his head. "We must obey our Lord, young man, not men. We are all sinners. Perhaps the Lord will do a work in their hearts." He added. "Give your enemy a cup of water and you will heap burning coals on his head." He smiled and looked at me over the rim of his classes. "Pray for those who despitefully use you. We pray, for God to forgive us our trespasses, and we must forgive others their trespasses against us. Jesus said if you do not forgive others, neither will your father in heaven forgive you. It is better to listen to Him than to trust in our feelings."

The pastor's words pricked at my heart, and I remembered that book again as well as my mother's words. The old preacher's sincerity impressed me. The worship service soon caught us all up. The church was a new experience for me.

Most of us were used to a formal worship. However, I saw that Pete and Kathy were right at home. I remembered then that they attended an AME church in Mechanicsburg. They were familiar with the style of worship, and they were into the worship as if they were at home.

In all the time I had known them I never thought of them as religious. Their enthusiastic involvement in the worship intrigued me. I wondered if their church at home was as open.

The service was lively and exciting, with everyone, except the most elderly, standing, dancing and clapping.

They raised their hands and prayed aloud, their eyes closed. I saw the joy on everyone's faces and felt the sincerity in the singing, which was loud and unrestrained. A lively choir in blue robes and gold mantles swayed and danced, and spontaneous prayers were called out by congregants, and the pastor.

Everyone sat and listened raptly as the preacher dramatically read from the bible, punctuated often by the congregants' comments.

"David tarried still at Jerusalem."

"Amen!"

"David sent messengers and took her"

"Oh Lord have mercy!"

"And she came in unto him, and he lay with her"

"Amen!"

I had to stifle a laugh at the awkward interruptions as they seemed inappropriate to events in the reading.

The pastor said, "Nathan told David a parable of a man who took his neighbor's sheep for his own pleasure and David said 'As the Lord liveth, the man that hath done this thing shall surely die'"

"Mercy, Mercy!"

"Nathan said to David, *Thou art the man...* David cried out, *I have sinned against the Lord.*"

"Amen brother!"

"And Nathan said unto David, the Lord also hath put away thy sin. Thou shalt not die."

"The Lord is great. Praise the Lord. Oh, Praise the Lord"

"Howbeit, because by this deed thou hast given great occasion to the enemies of the LORD to blaspheme."

"Lord have mercy on us for we have sinned!" The choir leader intoned at the end of the reading.

The preacher delivered a lively sermon condemning sin and debauchery in the flesh and calling down God's judgment on sinners saying, "Your sins will find you out!"

"Beware of pride my brothers and sisters and friends. David became puffed up and prideful and he forgot the Lord, The Lord who gave him everything. The Lord who raised him up. He forgot, what the lord giveth, the Lord can taketh away. Remember, brothers, sisters, everything we have, no matter how great or how small, it all came from the Lord, and we all need to remember Him and be thankful."

I squirmed, uncomfortable. I hoped my friends were ready to leave, but they all appeared to be engrossed in the sermon. No one seemed eager to leave and the preacher's dynamic and energetic speaking was impossible to ignore. His words stuck in my mind.

I saw Carol looking scared, tears rolling down her cheeks. I tried to get Connie's attention and she and Eleanor shushed me.

The preacher concluded, "We have *all* sinned, and we are *all* under God's Judgment because we have *all* violated God's commandment and brought reproach on the Lord. Nevertheless, there *is* help! God has sent a savior. David confessed his sin, and he received mercy. God is in the mercy business and everyone who repents and confesses Jesus and confesses their sins to Jesus *will* receive mercy. All their sins will be forgiven, and they will *all* be cast away into the deepest sea! Never to be remembered."

Carol was crying openly, her face streaked with tears. Chuck was sitting next to her, and he tried to put his arm around her, but she pushed him away. He looked confused as an older woman moved close to Carol, put her arm around her, and held her gently, patting her shoulder. A woman in the next pew gave her a tissue.

I was uncomfortable and relieved when the service ended. As we filed out, we received an invitation to stay for dinner. I was champing at the bit to get away, but the others eagerly accepted the invitation.

Eleanor said, "Carol is not finished yet, she's still talking to the ladies. We'll wait for her."

Pete said, "In the meantime we can get something to eat before heading home."

I looked for Carol and saw her inside, sitting in the pew with several women talking to her. I wondered if I should try to rescue her.

Heaps of food were provided, piled on tables under the trees beside the cemetery. Everyone sat around the tables in the church yard sharing in the feast. As was common in the old days the graveyard was next to the old church and some parishioners sat in lawn chairs under the trees among the markers at the edge of the burial ground. All my friends sat at a picnic table with the young people of the church while I reverted to type and hovered around the fringe. Connie tried to encourage me, but I was not comfortable.

Dennis was obviously not comfortable and kept looking toward the road as if he were eager to go. He became even more withdrawn than I often did, hovering far away from the crowd.

Carol finally came and joined us. She was positively radiant, in contrast to moments before.

I said, "Carol! Are you ok? You looked upset before."

"Yes!' She hollered, "*I'm Ok, now. Really, I'm ok. I got saved and now I'm really ok.*" I was taken aback by her answer.

"Saved, oh… *oh-kayee.*" I vacillated. I looked at Dennis and he shrugged.

Many of the young people hugged her enthusiastically. Dennis and Chuck *looked* as uncomfortable as I felt. Pete was smiling broadly and nodding approval.

Carol told us how the ladies and the pastor explained the gospel to her and that she prayed and confessed her sins to Jesus and asked him to come into her heart and save her. "And He did!" She exclaimed at last, "I feel like a new person!" She enthused, "I *am* a new person! I've been born again!"

Chuck acted like he was happy for her, but he was unusually quiet, and looked confused. Dennis and I were quiet; the whole business was weird to us. Dennis and his family were not religious people at all, and he left ahead of the rest of us. "I'll see you back at the house." He mumbled to me and headed off down the road. I was tempted to go with him, but I wanted to be with Connie.

The festivities wound down, but Carol did not. As we walked back to the house, she continued to go on, repeating her story. After about the third or fourth time that she spoke to me about getting saved and being born again I snapped at her. "Ok, ok. I get it! You've been born again. You're a new person. I don't need that crap! It seems to me you are the same loud talkative person who doesn't know when to shut up."

That dampened her enthusiasm, but only for a moment. Before long, she was talking again as the others eagerly listened. She did not speak to me again.

Connie grumbled, "That was rude, Michael." She would not let me put my arm around her or hold her hand.

"You don't think it's rude for her to keep on yammering about that stuff?"

"She's excited and she has every right to be. You should be glad for her. This is a big step in a person's life. The biggest."

"Yeah, well. I don't need it." I scoffed.

"We all need to get saved. To accept Jesus into our lives."

"Then why didn't you. Back there I mean."

"I am saved, Michael. I was saved when I was thirteen… at our church." She touched the cross around her neck.

"You sure didn't act saved last night."

She looked hurt as she stared at me, her lip quivering. Then she rejoined. "You are right. I acted badly. I'm sorry." She stared at the road as she walked, and she kept her distance from me. "But I did stop you." She muttered frostily, "I don't think I have that much to be ashamed of… I *did* stop you."

Eleanor, walking beside Connie, gave me a frosty look… I *felt* cold.

We were all quiet as we packed the carryall. I said to Connie, "Are you still planning to fly the plane home? Or have you changed your mind?"

"No, I haven't changed my mind. I'll fly the plane."

"You need to get to planning. Don't forget to check the weather."

"I know how to prepare a flight plan."

"Ok."

She went to make her preparations. The girls were cool to me all the way to the airport.

As we turned in at the airport entrance, Eleanor stared at a car that sped by, heading toward the beach. "I think my dad was in that car."

"You're feeling guilty for not calling your mom." Kathy suggested. "What would your dad be doing here?"

"Well, they couldn't find you all in Wildwood, so they came here." I chuckled. "And here we are leaving."

We all looked at each other and laughed.

Eleanor said. "I got so busy, I forgot. I'll call mom and let her know we're on our way home. I probably should not mention Dad."

Connie filed her flight plan and began inspecting the plane. We loaded up and took off. We all stopped for lunch at an airfield on Maryland's Eastern Shore near a crab fishery.

"We don't want a repeat of the church incident so why don't a couple of us go get the food and we can have a picnic here at the airfield." Eleanor suggested.

The fishery pier was a short walk away and Eleanor, Dennis and Chuck soon returned with crabs and drinks.

While they were gone, I sat next to Connie. She didn't look at me or say anything. I could feel her coolness. "I'm sorry. You are right... I should not have spouted off. You *did* the Christian thing, stopping me. I apologize. I *do* respect you for that. I guess I am not as fond of church or religion as you guys are."

"I often neglect my Christian teaching. I get caught up in having fun at school and stuff, I forget who I am. I forget Jesus." She was quiet. "But I would not be the person I am and could not make it through some days... *most* days without Jesus. When I forget him, I get in trouble."

"I don't know what to think. Mom is religious, but Dad is not. When I saw the way people acted at Mom's old church... just like those people in Cape May... I think maybe Dad is right. I do alright without God."

"Michael, you shouldn't say that. God helps us, even when we don't realize it. We need to always be thankful for him."

"I just don't feel it, Connie."

"Be careful you aren't like David in that sermon. Pride can deceive you."

"Now you sound like my mother. Can we not talk about this... please?"

After we arrived at Harrisburg I spoke to Carol, "Hey, I'm sorry. I apologize for being rude. I shouldn't be raining on your parade. I'm glad that you're happy."

"No problem. I guess I was coming on pretty strong. I did not mean to bother you." She gave me a hug and a kiss on the cheek. "I'm ok, and I'll be happy if you're ok. I will pray for you."

"Thanks." I smiled. "I'll be ok. I'll see you guys around. I guess it's back to school tomorrow. Exams are coming up and I have to get this plane back to Gifford's. Are you guys coming?"

Kathy came from the office to inform us that her cousin, who lives in Camp Hill, would pick up her and Pete. They left to wait for her cousin outside.

Back at Gifford's, Dennis, Chuck and I piled into Dennis's Chevy for the drive to York Landing. None of us were particularly religious and we made light of the day's events but quickly turned to other more interesting subjects.

"Tell me the truth Dennis. You guys are rebuilding that old plane, aren't you?"

"I guess you figured it out after all the noise down on the river last week."

"Yeah, the report of a plane crash was suspicious. Especially when they couldn't find any wreckage. What happened?"

"Let's go down to the island, Dennis. We can show him." Chuck said.

"Woody won't like it." Dennis said and smiled. "But what the heck."

We drove to York Landing and boarded Dennis's boat for the trip to Tanner Island.

CHAPTER 23

"Hi, Michael… Chuck." David greeted us at the barn. "Are you ok, Dennis? Where have you guys been all weekend."

"I'm Ok. We went down to Wildwood. We were on our way back and thought we would show Michael our, uh… project."

David shrugged, "Yeah, I guess it would be alright. Woody isn't here."

I was taken aback by what they showed me. "This isn't what I saw in the barn."

The engine was reclaimed from an airboat. It was mounted high on the back of a parasol wing with a pusher prop. The cockpit was forward of the wing right in the bow. "So, this is what you guys have been up to. I thought it was a J-3 or a Taylorcraft. Uh, why? I would have thought you could rebuild the plane. It looks like you tried to copy the Curtiss Flyer."

"Yeah, not quite." David laughed. "The old frame was J-3, but it was damaged. We could only use the wing and the tail. Most of the main frame from the cockpit forward was not salvageable."

"Whoever had it last must have crashed." Dennis shrugged. "We could not make a runway on the island without drawing attention and with the river right here, a seaplane seemed logical. Woody designed it to the Curtiss's design, but we changed it because we could not find another wing."

"Yeah, and why re-invent the wheel?" David said. "So, we designed our own version of Curtiss."

"You should have built the plane at Gifford's point. You would have had professional help and an inspector to check it out. The pond is big enough to land a small seaplane I think."

David shrugged. "We just wanted to do it ourselves."

Dennis explained, "We tried to test it Wednesday morning. We didn't think there would be anyone on the river mid-week and I tried to do a little test hop in it."

"Weren't you afraid of being seen by the Air Force?" I spoke.

"No, it was early, and we thought we'd be ok but that turned out to be the least of our worries." Dennis said. "I found it hard to control and I should have stopped, but the guys kept bugging me…"

"That was Woody, Dennis… not us." David protested.

"Yeah, uh, well, when I opened the throttle, it dragged to the right, and I shut it down. Everyone… er, Woody, was getting mad at the delay and I was afraid to keep going. But I didn't want to quit. That was a mistake… you know what Kelly says, if it feels wrong, stop."

"I thought that if I got it up on the step it would be ok. It felt ok at first and I thought it was going to work… then it went crazy. The wind hit me, I think. I lost control and I was all over the place… got turned around. Scared the hell out of me. I cut the engine before I did any damage… or hurt myself."

We watched Woody drive up from the Bailey bridge from the east shore.

Dennis said. "I told them something was wrong, and we needed to find out what, before anyone tried it again. Woody said I was scared, that I was chicken. We argued and I walked away. Now we don't know what we're going to do."

"Hey Dennis." Woody got out of his car. As usual he did not look happy. "I see you're back… and you brought your loser friend. Did you tell him about your big crash?"

"Yeah, he was telling me about *Woody's Folly*." I spoke. Woody and I never got along; he always seemed haughty, and I didn't know if it was me or if he was like that with everyone. I suspected everyone was beneath him in his mind.

"Woody's folly my fanny. He can't fly."

"I can fly better than you. I'm not the one who failed his test… twice." Woody looked as if he would bite someone. "*Your* airplane is not safe." Dennis retorted. "And I did not crash. I stopped *before* I crashed. It's not safe! You're the engineer. *Fix it!*"

"Baloney! It's no good after you wrecked it. Besides it is not my design, need I remind you? You guys changed it. I wanted to build the Curtiss Flyer."

"Yeah, but you went along with our suggestion, and you designed the modification… so now you want to deny it because it doesn't work? Figures." David said.

Dennis repeated, "It's not wrecked. I stopped before it got wrecked. Nothing's broke… especially my head.

"You're the genius… you figure it out and *you* fly it."

David muttered. "If he can pass his test."

Dennis said. "I'm out. I don't care if you think I'm chicken so save your breath. The floats are wrong… they drag in the water. It's unstable and a light wind will knock the plane off course."

I walked around studying the plane feeling a touch of envy. The plane appeared to be ok, except for the wing tip floats."

"Well *Hunter*? Does it meet with your approval?" Woody asked sarcastically.

"No. Dennis is right. The floats are too low… they will drag in the water. And maybe if you put a fairing in front of the rudder… I don't know if that would help with the wind. They help reduce drag though."

Woody said, "The plane has to float level in the water dufus."

"It has to be level during takeoff. It does not matter when it is sitting still on the water. Did you really fail your test?"

"The flight test." David said.

Woody scoffed. "It's none of your business how I did on my test."

"Eleanor and Connie passed. We shared the flying when we went down to Wildwood this weekend." The frown on his face deepened as the guys all tried stifling laughs. "But then you're right. This is none of my business." I turned away. Conflicting thoughts were churning in my head. I thought I would love to fly this plane. I said, "You guys never invited me to get involved and as far as I am concerned, I never saw this. As an apprentice mechanic, I would be bound to report you… if I saw this or knew what you were doing. Maybe I should."

"You were stuck up after you got your license and didn't think we were good enough for you." Woody sneered.

"*What?* Look who's calling the kettle black. You are the biggest snob in class, Woody. Every time I talked about flying, all I ever got from you was, oh you're a loser, or get lost dreamer. I kept to myself, because that's what you and everyone else wanted. You made that pretty clear... most of you. I asked you about this in March and you were all," I waved my hands wildly, *"Oh no, we aren't doing anything with that."* I looked around at the guys. No one would look at me. They Fidgeted and kept their eyes averted. "Are we done here Dennis? I'm ready to go." I headed for the boat.

Woody yelled. "You're still nothing but a loser... and a dreamer."

Someone muttered, "The country was built by dreamers." I smiled remembering Arnold.

"Hey. Come on, Michael." David followed me. "I'm sorry if we pushed you away... and for all that stuff last fall. But I... *we* could really use your help now. We would like you to help us... if you are willing."

"Yeah, Michael. We could use your help. You have experience working on planes as a mechanic." Chuck said. "We need someone with experience. We need you."

"I don't know. I would risk losing my license." The temptation was too much, pulling at my mind and my heart... I was still a dreamer. "What do you want *me* to do? It is pretty much done. All you have to do is figure out why it goes crazy. I don't know if it is as simple as the floats... or the fairing. It just may have been a combination of stuff."

"You help us figure it out... and you will be the first to fly it. You have more experience." Dennis said, "You would be our inspector."

"Well, I don't know about that." I laughed.

"Yeah, come on, Michael. We really do need your help." David said. "We don't want to waste all this effort, time and money. I am sure it will fly given half a chance."

"Don't you guys want to fly it? You put all the work into it."

I saw Woody brooding as he studied the airplane. He appeared not to be listening.

"Yeah, you can check it out and then we can take turns if it works." Dennis said.

I laughed. "Yeah, but where are we going to fly it? We can't do it on the river."

Yeah, I thought; I can test it and if I crash and kill myself then no loss, right? In spite of my misgivings, the craving was eating at me. I was still a dreamer. Woody was not far wrong. When I wrote that book report I dreamed of flying a Curtiss airplane and here was my dream staring me in the face. This excited me.

And... this was the first time I was ever invited to be a part of their plans. Participating in the rifle and pilot's clubs was still all an individual thing, in spite of competing as a team. I was never really *in* with the guys. That was the clincher.

"We could take it down to the bay near Havre De Grace." David suggested.

I thought aloud. "That is too near a populated area. Dan Kelly uses a little field on the east shore near Betterton. I don't think he is using it this year. He has several shows in Ohio, and he will be gone for most of the month. There is a Quonset hut hangar near the water and a beach. You can reach the water easy."

With the girls showing interest in me early in the year and now the guys asking for my help, I was hooked. Asking me, Michael Hunter, the dreamer, for help. I felt proud. I was finally in with the guys! I felt important. All the work, learning to fly, learning mechanics were all paying off. I was not just in with them… they looked up to me… or so I told myself. They even depended on me. They *needed* me. My self-esteem was in the clouds. I was flying high, in more ways than I could count.

I was distracted as I studied for final exams and Dad wondered, "What's going on with you, Michael? You seem more distracted than usual. I haven't seen you this quiet since you were in eighth grade. Daydreaming again?"

"No." I grimaced. "It's just the finals. You know me and math. I've done so well until now… I don't want to blow it at the finish line."

"You have been out, spending more time with your friends. I haven't seen you so interested in your classmates before." Mom said.

"Yeah, we are, uh studying together. Everyone is worried about the finals."

"Oh?" Dad had a skeptical look, his eyes narrowed suspiciously. "Are these the same guys that avoided you most of the time? And, uh, who made so much trouble for you?" Dad was still reluctant to talk about the affair of November. It was still a thorn in our relationship.

"Well, we just decided to let bygones be bygones. We are all in the same boat now… looking to get good grades and get out of school. Everyone is excited and distracted… excited by what is to come next."

"I think it's good that you can forgive them, Michael, that's a very Christian thing to do." Mom said. "I am glad you are finally getting involved with your classmates."

"I don't know." Dad persisted. "I would be suspicious of their sudden interest. You are always warning him of letting his pride take him."

I was thinking that Dad had a problem with his own pride, and I almost bit my tongue trying not to say something nasty. "I think it's about time they gave me what's due. We have about two weeks left and I intend to enjoy their respect as long as I can. Then I am out of here and will probably never see them again."

"Your father is right about pride. Don't let your pride deceive you. I know the bible says to forgive others and I am happy you have done that, but just be careful you don't give them occasion to take advantage of you."

The way they were talking I wondered if they had heard something, but I dismissed that as nerves. Certainly, if they knew about the plane they would say so.

CHAPTER 24

Commander McCormick was promoted to Captain and received orders to a ship on the west coast and after the graduation rite, my father drove Ian to the Air Force Base to catch a flight to the west coast. Connie and her mother were to follow later. After Elizabeth drove us all home. Mom and Elizabeth decided to visit for a while.

Connie said, "Mom, Michael and I want to spend some time together. Could I borrow the car?"

"Well, I don't know. How am I going to get home, sweetheart?"

"We'll be back before midnight, and Dad will probably be back before that."

"Ok, just be careful, you two." Elizabeth said.

We drove to the River Park by the boat launch ramp on the river. There were a few people preparing to go out to their cabins on the islands. We strolled hand in hand through the park.

We played around in the children's playground. We were like children whirling about on the roundabout and staggered around dizzily after. The few patrons in the park laughed at our childish playing. But the park soon emptied, and we had it to ourselves. We took another whirl on the apparatus and staggered down along the river embankment and almost fell in. We finally settled in the long grass, laughing and giggling.

We lay close together looking up at the moon and the stars.

"Well, I guess it's all over, isn't it?" I spoke.

"No, it is just beginning, Michael." Connie rolled over and leaned on my chest. "We have life ahead of us."

"Yeah, but I wonder if our paths will ever cross again." I wrapped my arms around her.

"Boy, are you a party pooper." She touched my cheek. "I think it is all so exciting. I am off to college, and you are going into the Navy." She looked doubtful. "You are still going to join up, aren't you? That should excite you."

"Oh, it does. I will probably sign up later in June. I hope I can get into aircraft mechanics."

"Gee why am I not surprised?" She laughed.

"But you'll be off to some university, and I may never see you again. Where are you going anyway?"

"Eastern Oregon... business major."

"Sounds boring."

"Noo." She poked me in the ribs. "Not boring."

"So, I guess we will not see each other again after tonight... unless we go to class reunions."

She turned her nose up. "Class reunions? I don't know. I will be glad to get away from here and I thought you were eager to get out of here too."

"I am. You are the only good thing I can think of from this school." I wrapped my arms around her and pulled her close. We kissed. It started as a gentle buss but quickly turned passionate.

She was thoughtful for a moment. "Michael, this may be the last we will ever see of each other."

"Now who's the party pooper?"

She looked sad and I held her close, thinking about that. That threatened to put a damper on the evening, but we held each other tightly, snuggling close, not wanting the evening to end.

The warmth of the spring evening, cuddling and kissing, was so pleasurable that we quickly became lost in the moment. There was no one else in the world, no past, no future… just us, the here and now… just us. Caught up in our passion, kissing and caressing. We were overcome by our emotions… by our feelings… our passion took wings… it knew no bounds and time stood still. We were carried far away from the world. We fell asleep, wrapped in each other's arms, exhausted.

I woke up suddenly and realized it was late, getting on toward morning. I woke Connie up.

"Oh my god. I'm in trouble. I have to get ready to leave. Mother and I must catch a flight today. She's going to kill me. I was going to have the car back by midnight."

As we straightened our clothes Connie seemed to become troubled. I thought she was crying but she kept her back turned and her face hidden as she finished adjusting her clothes. "Are you ok, Connie?"

"Y-yes." She did not sound Ok. I could tell she was not happy. She spoke again. "I–I. We shouldn't… no. I'm… ok. We have to go. *Where is my purse*… and the keys?" She grabbed up her purse and hurried to the car. I followed, a troubled feeling growing inside, as if the night never happened. I thought we should be happy but there was a sense of gloom and doom. I thought she was deliberately not looking at me... it occurred to me, *she was ashamed.*

I suspected... I thought I knew what was bothering her. The problem was spiritual, and I felt a sense of resentment... toward God. I was sure that was it, but I was hardly the person to discuss spiritual things. When I pressed her for answers, she was evasive and abruptly changed the subject. "Some of the girls were saying that the boys tried to fly a home built airplane down on Tanner Island. I heard them talking about rebuilding that wreck in the barn... the one you saw when you were there. The girls said it crashed. That was apparently what all the commotion was about last week. I hope no one was hurt."

"Oh? Uh, yeah." I wondered who had been talking. "Dennis tried to fly it, but it did not run right, and he stopped before anything happened. He didn't crash though."

"Oh, good for him." She looked at me sharply. "Michael, tell me you are not involved with that?"

Her abruptness bothered me. "I wasn't then, but we are going to try it again, but not on the river." I was not sure I should be telling her that and at once regretted it.

She looked at me. "You have got to be kidding me. Michael, tell me you are not going to fly that... that piece of junk." Her voice was rising.

"It's not a piece of junk, Connie."

"You can't fly it. It almost killed Dennis. Why would you?"

"It did not *almost kill Dennis.* He stopped the test when he sensed something was wrong. That's what tests are for."

"Even so, you can't fly it. If you're caught you will lose your license. After all the work you've done, why risk it? You will probably lose your mechanics license too. Michael, you can't throw everything away. You should not let them talk you into anything. You don't owe them anything. They're only using you." The tone of her voice and the intensity of her speech irritated me. I became defensive and my irritation overflowed into my voice as it rose, like it did when I was agitated. I sounded whiney. The magic of the evening was ebbing quickly if it was not already gone.

"They are *not* using me. I chose... I *want* to be involved."

"But Michael, flying that... that thing is not right... it's not safe."

"I promised to help. Anyway, just knowing about it makes me involved. I have to help make it work. I can make sure no one gets killed." I was trying to convince myself and my anger grew the more she argued. "Even if I quit now, someone else will fly it. I promised them and I can't go back on my promise."

"What about you? *You* could get killed."

"I don't think so. It is a good design. It just needed some adjustments... to the floats. They were..."

"Michael you can't. It's foolish. It's totally stupid." She became loud; emotional, and almost drove off the road in her zeal.

"Hey! Watch what you are doing. You'll kill us both. If you can't keep your head maybe I should drive." We just missed a string of mail boxes and she swerved all over the road for a bit which only got my pulse going.

"Maybe a broken arm or leg will keep you from flying that piece of junk. You are being stupid Michael. I never thought you were stupid."

"So now I'm stupid." My resentment took control. "Don't talk down to me. I'm not your husband… or your brother. *I'm going to do this. I'm committed to it.*" The magic of the evening disappeared in a flood of anger.

"You *should* be committed. You're acting crazy. You're only doing this to be popular with the guys. It's just stupid pride." She retorted. "And stop yelling."

"You stop yelling." We were degenerating into childishness. *"You sound like my mother. My pride is fine. Maybe you should watch your pride."* I yelled. *"And stop calling me stupid. Is that really what you think of me?"*

"I never did before now. If it walks like a duck and *quacks like a* duck, then it must be a…"

"Shut up and let me out here."

"Michael, we are not close to your home."

"Let me out… now!" I screamed. I knew my voice was rising and whiney, but I didn't care. "I don't want to listen to any more of your crap." I unlatched the door as if I would jump out.

"Ok. Have it your way. You… you…" She slammed on the brakes.

"Go ahead. Call me stupid one more time." I opened the door abruptly and jumped out before the car was completely stopped and almost fell into the roadside ditch.

"Michael, wait… please. I thought we were friends." She got out as I slammed the door and started to walk away. "Doesn't our friendship mean anything? After what we have been through together… and after tonight… I'm asking… begging you not to do this Michael, please. For me."

I paused and answered. "Our friendship is important, but I can't turn my back on my friends, especially Dennis… not even for you. He was my friend long before you. Don't ask me to break my promise to him. It won't end the test."

"Yes, I am asking you to break your promise."

"You want me to break a promise? You're pretty fickle when it comes to promises aren't you?"

She started to cry as she pleaded, "Michael, please, if you want to save his life call the FAA. They will stop this madness and you will save his life. Maybe I will."

"Well, I guess I know where I really stand with you. You go ahead. Call them. I *am* going to fly that airplane." I turned and stomped off up the road. Somewhere inside I felt a door slamming shut.

She yelled. "Well, maybe I *will* call them." She was crying. "You're going to get yourself killed. Don't expect me to come to your funeral." She slammed the door and drove into a driveway to turn around. She peeled out swerving all over the road. For a moment I worried as she just missed a telephone pole… just a moment.

The moment of concern was inundated by bitterness. I fumed as I walked the last mile home. Who does she think she is? That we're married because we had sex? Let her call the FAA. She doesn't know where we are going. She's wrong. I can fly it. I *will* fly it. She'll see.

It was close to sunrise when I arrived home. Everyone was in bed, so I changed my clothes, left a note telling Mom and Dad that I was spending the weekend at Gifford's Park with some of the guys. I met Dennis in York Landing near the memorial. I left the truck at Dietrich's, and we used his car to go to Maryland.

CHAPTER 25

Dennis and I arrived at the airfield in Maryland to find the guys assembling the airplane. I was wary as I watched the guys work. "I am not sure I want to fly an airplane assembled by a bunch of drunks."

"We are not drunk." David said, "While you lazy bums were sleeping… or making out with the girls, we were working."

"*That* I would have to see to believe." Dennis said.

"Which… making out, or working?" Chuck said.

Dennis laughed. "Either one."

David said. "We left right after graduation and hauled the plane down here in the horse trailer last night."

Chuck said. "We loaded the plane in Johnny Smyth's big horse trailer Thursday night. There was no time for drinking. We were dead tired and hit the sack as soon as we got here."

"I see a lot of beer cans. If you're not drunk, you're all probably suffering from hangovers… same difference."

David said. "They're not ours. Are you sure this place is secure? It looks like it gets a lot of use."

Woody was ignored as he hovered around. He was unusually quiet. That should have been a warning, but I guess we were all glad for the silence. He did seem sullen, and his involvement was lackluster at best. I thought maybe he wished he was somewhere else.

The airplane was completely assembled, and we stopped to have a late lunch before testing the engine. I borrowed a two way radio from the shop at Harrisburg without telling Crombie. We installed the radio and tested it. Everything seemed ready by late afternoon, and we pushed the airplane to the water. With the plane held level both floats now just cleared the water. It was late in the afternoon when I took it out and taxied around on the bay. I taxied at high speed but did not try to lift off. My heart was eager to fly. It came up onto the step smoothly and I could hold it on a straight line. I was tempted to lift off, but the feelings were mixed with fear and anticipation and after the busy night and day, I wanted to be rested so I let my doubts dictate my actions. I took a breath, relaxed and took the plane back to the beach. We had all day tomorrow to fly around, no need to rush.

Woody woke up and complained about the delay. I spoke. "I am flying this plane, and I will decide if it is safe. It's my ass on the line. I'll take all the time I need." He was not happy, that was obvious.

It was getting late, and we relaxed and enjoyed the evening. Some of the guys went for a swim. Then we had a bar-b-q and beer, but I settled for a coke.

"Take it easy with that stuff, guys." Dennis warned, "We don't want anyone drunk… or with a hangover in the morning."

"Yeh," I said. "Save it for the celebration after." I heard some mutterings about me being bossy. I did not say anything. Of course I was being bossy. After all I was going to fly the plane, not them.

All evening the guys, one after the other, would go over and touch our toy, dreaming about flying it.

"Hey, has anyone seen Woody?" Dennis asked.

David answered, "I think he went to bed early. He does that at home I hear."

An hour later Chuck came from where we parked our cars. "Hey guys. Woody's car is gone."

David worried, "Oh crap. He's going to blow the whistle."

Dennis said, "You think he would do that? Maybe he came along to find out where we were flying it."

We were all quiet for the next hour or so. But as we talked about the plane and the impending test, we became more excited. As the evening progressed and after a few more burgers and beers, Woody was forgotten. We enjoyed the spring evening; anticipating a busy and exciting day tomorrow.

After breakfast we pushed the plane to the water, and I taxied up the river to takeoff into the wind. I opened the throttle and as the speed increased, I pulled back on the stick. The plane came up smoothly onto the step; I held the wings level, the floats clear of the water.

I felt the rush as the speed increased, the wind blowing in my face and the water rushing past sent my pulse into overtime. I opened the throttle all the way and shouted into the microphone. "This is great guys!" I did not hear a reply.

As I came by the dock I pulled back on the stick and the airplane lifted off from the water. I was flying and it felt good, better than I had thought. I circled and flew back past the landing. I could see the guys on the dock jumping and punching the air. I began a series of turning maneuvers making level passes, performing tight turns, and calling out reports over the radio. I still did not hear any reply and assumed the radio was not working.

I climbed high over Chesapeake Bay. I saw a freighter heading up, probably to the Chesapeake-Delaware canal. A large white craft was heading up the bay toward the east shore. I was enjoying the view; I could see across the bay to the army proving grounds just two miles away. I needed to stay away from there; the army would not like strange planes flying too close. I turned back toward the Eastern shore.

While doing climbing turns, I was in a climbing turn and the airplane stalled and went into a spin. I brought it out of the spin ok, but it gave me a fright. When I leveled off, I was just feet off the water. Shaken, I thought of ending the test, but I decided to climb higher and do a stall from what I thought would be a safer altitude.

I announced my intention over the radio and still did not hear a reply. I increased the power to climb and headed out over the bay. I turned back toward the shore at 5000 feet. Everything looked the same as I searched for the airstrip. I saw a large white boat at a dock and thought I was out of position. I scanned the shore looking for the Quonset hut. My eyes passed over it but because of the boat at the dock I did not think that was the right place and for a moment I panicked, thinking maybe I had become disoriented. That was easy to do while flying and turning a lot. I scanned the shore again more carefully and realized that the boat was at our dock.

Warning bells went off in my head. Oh crap, is that a Coast Guard cutter? Immediately I thought of Connie, *you're going to get caught and go to jail.* I supposed that I could just fly away and land up the bay somewhere and chuckled at the thought. As I came near to the shore I saw the flashing lights near the Quonset hut. I muttered, "She did it. She called the FAA." Resentment filled me. "I'll show her."

I pulled back on the stick and the speed dropped dramatically. The plane mushed and I worked the rudder vigorously trying to keep my heading as the plane began to fall. The right pedal jammed, and the airplane fell into a spin. *Oh crap.*

I kicked at the rudder pedal to no avail. Frantic, I bent down and after several hard tugs, loosened the pedal. When I straightened up, the nose of the plane had come up. The plane was in a flat spin! That is not good.

The controls had no effect. My heart pounded against my ribs and my stomach felt loose… it felt like my heart and my breakfast wanted to abandon ship. A feeling of déjà vu grew… from a long-forgotten dream. I applied full power but that only seemed to increase the spin. I cut the power.

To shift my weight forward and get the nose down I unbuckled my seat belt and, gripping the edge of the cockpit, I leaned forward over the windshield. The nose dropped abruptly with the shift of weight, and I was almost catapulted out of the cockpit. I gripped the edge of the cockpit in a panic and finally pulled myself back inside. Somehow, I managed to fasten the seatbelt. It seemed like an eternity, but it was only seconds. The nose was down but I was still spinning. I pushed on the rudder to stop the spin and pulled back gently on the stick to level the plane. I saw that the water seemed awfully close. I was *really* low, and I pulled back hard and pushed the throttle to maximum. The engine whined and the wings creaked and moaned with the stress. I expected the plane to stall or the wings to come off. Either way I was going to hit the water. My heart raced.

As the nose came up and the speed increased, a loud *crack* came from the wings. I heard a loud popping sound come from the left wing and a huge swath of fabric came off and trailed from the wing. The airplane was yanked to the left by the drag, and I pushed hard right on the rudder hoping it did not jam again. The turn stopped and the airplane was moving forward and picking up speed when it hit the water and skipped. I was driven down into the canvass seat, rattling my teeth. I felt a jar in my head and neck, and I wondered if I broke my neck. I did not feel any pain though the canvass seat ripped under me. I was dazed; my heart was racing as I realized my helplessness. I was not in control. I could die any minute. I thought of my mother and her warnings.

A huge spray of water engulfed the plane as it skipped across the water and pulled left. My efforts to straighten were useless as the trees on the shore rapidly approached. I was along for the ride, and everything seemed to happen in slow motion. The airplane settled sideways, struck the water again and the wing dipped, jerked the machine violently, and spun it around. The plane plowed backwards into the reeds along the shore.

Everything was quiet and still. I opened my eyes… *I'm alive!* I felt a rumbling in my stomach. I felt water on the cockpit floor. *Oh god, I'm sinking.* I fumbled with the belt buckle and when I tried to get out of the cockpit, the radio cord stopped me. In a panic I tore it from the panel and dove out of the plane, plunging head first into the water. I swallowed the bay water at the same time my stomach tried to empty itself. I was choking on bile and water in a panic.

Rough hands seized me and pulled me out of the water. I was lying on the shore retching and trying to breathe, and someone was standing over me pounding my back. I heard a man's voice say. "He's alive. He'll be ok."

A crowd of uniformed men, cops, Coast Guardsmen and army, surrounded me.

"He'll be all right." One of the guardsmen, a corpsman, pronounced again.

An Army officer commanded. "Get him on the boat."

A couple of soldiers seized me and roughly carried me to the cutter; my feet did not want to work, and they dragged on the deck. I could feel them, but I felt weak.

I was examined again and pronounced alive and shoved into a locked room. There was a babble of voices outside. I could not understand any of it. Everything was in a haze much like I experienced when John ran into me; that seemed so long ago. I was wondering if I had a head injury, though I did not feel any pain, just a lot of confusion. My fears grew as the boat sped across the bay.

We arrived at the Aberdeen Army base where I was loaded into an ambulance. At a clinic or a hospital, a doctor pronounced me alive and healthy with only bruises for my misfortune. My pleasure at being pronounced alive and healthy withered when, roughly handled, I found myself in a small empty room by myself.

I asked, "What's happening. Where are my friends?"

An army sergeant answered roughly. "Shut up boy. We will ask the questions and you will answer when ordered. For now, be silent!"

"Yeah? So far no one has said… or asked me…" A whack on the head ended my speech.

My captors were not gentle. Two men, the Sergeant and a Captain, did not hesitate to grab me and shake me.

The sergeant handled the rough stuff while the officer asked questions. He hit hard enough to convince me to do as they said… I shut up. I was still confused from the crash and being hit on the head again did not help.

My prison held a table, a couple of chairs and no windows. My tormentors asked for my name, address, and parents' names, which I gladly gave, hoping that would get me out of there sooner. It would not be soon enough. They continued their rough interrogation.

"Who are you working for? Why were you flying around over the base?"

"I wasn't over the base…"

"You were in restricted airspace, boy. What were you doing?"

"We–we were just testing the plane. The guys built it"

"Why? Did you build it to spy on the base?"

"Spy? No-no, we were just having fun…."

"Fun? So, you think it is *fun* to spy on the US Army."

"N-no. Spy… *ha-ha-ha*... you think we were spying? We are just kids… *ha-ha*... we aren't spies."

One of the men smacked me on the side of the head and bent down close to my face and yelled… *he yelled*…right in my ear. *"So, you think its funny spying on the United States Army, do you?"* I almost peed myself.

The captain leaned across the table and yelled. *"Maybe spending the rest of your life in prison for spying won't be so funny."*

The sergeant muttered, "They give spies the electric chair don't they, Captain."

"Yes. They do." The captain glared at me.

That got my attention. Then I peed my pants. The men jumped back cursing. All I could think about at that moment was that I would never see my parents again.

I remembered hearing that the Aberdeen Proving ground was testing some top secret stuff and experimenting with gas and chemicals; and here I was, flying around over the bay close to the base. God, I thought, they think I was spying.

I started crying. "We weren't doing anything wrong. We aren't spies."

The men backed off shortly, and had some soldiers take me to the bathroom to clean up. They gave me a pair of pants that were way too big. I felt stupid enough as it was.

FAA agents came to interrogate me about the airplane. They were gentler than the soldiers and I ventured to ask about the other guys. But they told me not to worry about them. "You are in more trouble than them. You have plenty on your own plate to worry about. The army is still not so sure about you."

"Why am I in more trouble? *They* built the airplane. I only…"

"But *you* flew it. You are the only one with a license. The others are only students… *and* you are a licensed mechanic. It is not going to go well for you. Mark my words."

I heard them talking to the Army officers. They were reluctant to pass it off as just a high school prank. However, the FAA agent apparently won the debate. I was only a *little* relieved that they decided that I was not a spy.

I was left alone and as time passed, I got the shakes as I relived the crash and thought of how close I came to dying. It was all catching up to me and I felt sick… nauseous.

In my solitude I began to turn my thoughts to Connie to avoid thinking of the crash and the aftermath. That did not help. I became increasingly bitter toward her. I blamed her for my situation. I told myself… convinced myself that it was all her fault. I tried to get some sleep, but I couldn't sleep, my thoughts jumping from fears to doubts, to bitter thoughts, and hatred. I just wanted to see my mother. I just wanted to go home. I couldn't keep from crying.

Klienfeldt arrived Monday afternoon with Mom and Dad. "Well, young man, you've gotten yourself in some trouble now."

"No one will tell me anything." I was shaking and hungry.

"You are charged with making an unauthorized flight in an uncertified plane and endangering yourself and others to mention just few."

"I wasn't endangering others. I was the only one in the plane…"

"Michael, it would be a good idea for you to keep quiet." Dad warned. "You are in a lot of trouble, and it is not going to go away this time."

"But…"

"Michael." Mom spoke sharply. "Shut up and listen. You could have been killed. Just shut up and don't talk. We are relieved that you are alive and were not injured. But that is the *only* good thing from all of this. Be quiet. I will not tell you again."

Klienfeldt said. "As it stands right now your license is suspended and you are not permitted to be around airplanes or airports." I began to protest but Klienfeldt held his hand up while Mom and Dad glared at me. "We will have to wait for an official hearing to learn the full extent of the damages. As it is, you may go home with your parents. There is nothing more to be done here."

Dad would not talk to me all the way home, but Mom took me to task. "I warned you about letting your pride rule your head. You need to learn responsibility. This is what I was afraid of, taking on too much too soon. You have a long life ahead… hopefully. Pride goes before the fall. You worked so hard and achieved so much and it only took a moment… a foolish decision, to lose it all."

"I haven't lost it all, Mom."

"Don't kid yourself young man. You are going to be thinking about this week for a long time to come. Don't think you are going to get off lightly. That's your pride talking."

I went to Harrisburg Airport later in the week. When I entered the hangar, Mister Keith, the chief mechanic yelled at me. *"Hey you!* What are you doing here? You cannot be here. Get out! Now!"

"But I…"

"Out! Now!"

Kelly came from the lounge. "Michael, you have to leave. You can't be here. I do not want you here. Get out."

Kim followed, glaring angrily at me. Kelly said. "What did you do you little fool? I trusted you. You almost got Doug fired. He's under investigation because of that radio you stole." I tried to protest. "Yes, stole. You are lucky you are not charged for that.

"You had good potential, but you let it go to your head. I'm done with you. I don't want to see you around here anymore. Now, get out!" He pushed me toward the door.

"Hey stop pushing. You can't do this."

"Oh yes, I can. Do you want me to call security?"

Kim said. "You leave now, or I will give you a lesson you not soon forget."

CHAPTER 26

Barely a week passed before we received a summons to the FAA in Baltimore. All of the boys lost their student privileges.

The judge announced, "Michael Hunter, you are a special case in this event. You are a licensed pilot as well as an apprentice mechanic. Your Pilot's license is suspended for two years.

"Further, you are suspended and prohibited from working as a mechanic. You may reapply for your mechanic's license in five years. Your application will be taken under consideration at that time... there is no guarantee it will be restored. That depends on you. Keep your nose clean and you may eventually get into the aviation trade."

"I don't understand. I did not hurt anyone. The state and local police couldn't charge us with anything." I protested bitterly.

"Young man, the airways are governed by federal government regulations. As a certified pilot, and an apprentice mechanic, you are obliged to follow those regulations. They have been made for a reason. You seem to think that you are above the rules. You are fortunate that you are not charged with stealing the radio. You need to re- think your attitude and be glad your suspension is not permanent. This proceeding is adjourned."

The week dragged after Baltimore. Dietrich let me work longer hours now that I was out of school. I had lots of time on my hands and the boating season was in full swing. I had little to do in the evening.

Of course I did not work at Collins garage, and I could not go near an airport. I brooded in my workshop at home.

I did not see or hear from any of the other guys after Baltimore. I was disappointed that Dennis, my longtime friend, did not call. I decided that since I was not important anymore, they did not want anything to do with me. I did not want to think that they were just using me, because that would make my father, my mother and Connie right… and me wrong. I just did not want to concede that I had done anything wrong. After all, I did not hurt anyone; I did not steal anything I only borrowed the radio… I intended to return it. *Why was I being made the scapegoat? I did not hurt anyone.* The judge's words echoed in my mind, but I ignored them.

I was alone in my hobby shop in the basement, brooding and wondering about my future. I was not sure about enlisting in the navy. I was afraid they would not let me enlist now. Everything I worked for the last two years was ruined… because of Connie I was telling myself… that's what I wanted to believe. It was all her fault, I kept telling myself and I began to believe that.

My mother was frustrated; she repeatedly reminded me, "You better grow up young man and face reality. You are your own worst enemy right now." But my reality was what I made it. Dreaming was my specialty; that and model building.

I tried to work up the desire to finish the model of a Baltimore Privateer that I had begun building from scratch four years ago. It took a lot of careful fine work, assembling each small part by hand from scratch. I had neglected it for a long time, and it only required a few minor touches to be complete. It was my best effort by far, in my model building career. Everyone said it was magnificent.

"Michael?" Connie called from the stairs.

"What are *you* doing here?" I snapped bitterly.

"Your mother said you were here." she said quietly. "Mom and I came back to finish up with the house. We are leaving for Seattle today and I wanted to…"

"I don't care what you want. I do not want to see you or talk to you. Go away."

"Michael, please don't be angry. I…"

"Don't be angry?" I bellowed. My anger boiled over. Here was the object of my anger, the cause of all my problems. "You cost me everything and now you just waltz in here as if nothing happened? Do you think if you just give a clever smile everything will be alright? Well, it won't. *Get out! I don't ever want to see you.*"

Her voice rose at the accusation. "I cost you… what are you talking about? I did not make you fly that thing. I told you this would happen. I told you…"

"Yeah. Yeah. You told me. You are good at *telling*. Martha has nothing on you." I jumped up and almost knocked the model over. She jumped. My face was hot as my temper rose, I screeched, *"You had to go and tell! It would have been all right, but you snitched. The test went fine. I didn't get hurt and no one had to know."*

She shouted. *"I did not snitch on you. And the test did not go fine. You crashed you fool, and almost killed yourself."*

"NO!" I pounded my fist on the bench. The model bounced and almost fell over. Connie glanced at it and appeared alarmed. I modulated my voice and pointed my finger at her face. "That big mouth of yours was always making trouble. The teachers had you pegged. You were always talking about everything and everybody. You've got Martha and Wilson and those old cronies beat by miles." I bumped into airplane models hanging from the rafters as I gestured wildly with my hands and narrowly missed the ship again.

"Michael, watch what you're doing you're going to knock the mod…"

"This?" I swept the magnificent model off the table and flung it across the rec room.

"Michael!" Her mouth open, Connie barely avoided the ship as it flew past her head and shattered against the wall. Pieces flew everywhere in the rec room and lounge. I felt a twinge of regret, but I quickly blamed her for that too.

"You ruin everything. You ruined my life!" I stepped toward her, waving my arms. She backed away, her eyes wide with fear.

"Michael, stop."

"You betrayed me!" I shrieked. The blood rushing to my head was making my head and my eyes hurt.

"I did not betray you!" She retorted. *"You made your own bed. I did not make you fly that plane. You are trying to blame others for your stupidity. I am not to blame…"*

"Yeah. Yeah. There you go with the stupidity again. You're not to blame. When you get all knocked up," I waved my hands furiously, "you won't be to blame for that either."

She sputtered. *"You... you filthy pig."* She took a breath and growled. *"It's a sure bet you will never be to blame for that."*

"I'll tell the guys they didn't miss anything." I waved at her dismissively and started to turn away. But her voice dripping with contempt, she stepped up close, right in my face.

She sneered, *"You liked it."*

"It was a wasted evening." I spoke softly, not trying to conceal my scorn. "I should have taken a shower."

"You *are* a loser. John was right. You are a *stupid* loser! You are just like Mac. A loud mouth arrogant bully, full of yourself. But really, you are nothing. You are no better than Terry…"

"Yeah—yeah. *Terry*. Now we know. You had everyone fooled with your goody-two-shoes act. Now we know.

I was not the first; Terry plowed that field…" I reeled from her punch. I could not believe she actually punched me. I took a couple of steps back as she tried to hit me again. I blocked her and tried to hit her, but she got her arm up and blocked me. I grabbed her by the neck of her sweater; I saw red as I glared at her, my face was hot with the blood rushing to my head and her face became a blur. I hesitated as I felt dizzy, and a haze passed in front of my eyes. She brought her knee up catching me in the groin. I almost fell from the pain, and she grabbed my arm, bent the wrist back sharply, loosening my grip, twisted and pulled me over her hip and threw me onto the floor.

She screamed. *"Show me how much of a man you are, Michael."* Her voice dripped with loathing; tears streaked her face. *"I thought you were different. I—I thought that I loved..."*

I leaped up and went after her. She stumbled over a coffee table and fell back onto the couch. I was on top of her grabbing her around the throat. Her eyes were wide with terror as I began to tighten my grip.

Something stopped me. My hands froze as she abruptly relaxed. I saw a tear in her eye, and she gasped something inaudible. The look in her eyes, not terror, but sadness... pity, caused me to relax my grip. She seemed resigned to whatever would happen; she stopped struggling.

She spoke again but I did not understand. "What..." I hesitated and drew back.

"I love you and I forgive you." She rasped.

The look in her eyes and her words penetrated the rage and I stumbled back. I rubbed my head and my eyes. *What am I doing? Why? I love... loved her.* My head was hurting, and I grasped my head trying to make the pain go away. What am I doing? She rubbed her throat as I stared, confused, and horrified at what I had done. *No! No! This isn't right...*

Mom's broom landed on my shoulders with a smack. *"You animal."* She screamed, *"Get away from her! Get out!"* I fell back across the room. Mom stood between me and Connie, tears streaking her face, as she waved the broom at me like she was trying to smack an insect... a spider. "Get out! You monster. Get out!" I fled out the basement door to the back yard. I heard Mom yell. "And don't you come back until you can act civilized. I pray that God gives you a good smack in the head, Michael. God knows you need it."

CHAPTER 27

I wandered around the back yard confused. My head was spinning. I couldn't think. I had to get away. I did not have the keys for the truck, and the scooter was at Dietrich's. I found my old bike against the tool shed and headed for the road to York Landing. I heard Connie's car start and my mother calling out to her. Connie sped out of the drive onto the road without stopping. Fortunately, there was no traffic other than me. The way she peeled out and raced up the road toward me, I thought for a moment that she was going to run me down. I turned off onto a tractor path and she sped past heading toward her home in York Landing.

I came back out onto the road and looked back at our house. My mother was standing on the veranda at the rail. I thought about going back but her last words were ringing in my head. I watched as she sat down on the veranda and leaned back against the wall. Even from a distance I could sense an air of sadness or despair.

I headed down a side road and lost track of time as I rode the back roads, wandering aimlessly, overwhelmed with confused thoughts of rage, sadness, guilt, anger, fear… utter confusion.

I stopped at an old cemetery to rest. I did not know what to do or where to go. My mind raced, jumping from one disturbing thought to another. *What happened? What did I do?* I made excuses, dismissed them and came up with new ones with no satisfaction; only more confusion. I sat by an old tombstone. I needed to blame someone; anyone but me; but it kept coming back to me. It was my fault. *No! It was*

Connie's fault. But Connie did not fly the plane. She did not make me fly it. That was *my* choice. It was not her fault that it crashed. But it was her fault that I lost my license, *wasn't it? No! I broke the rules*. I *knew* that I was breaking the law. It was my pride just like Mom kept warning me! I put my face in my hands and began to cry.

My thoughts dwelled for a moment on the brawl. I could not believe that I wanted to hurt her. *Oh God! What was I thinking? What's happening to me?* I leaned back against the tombstone and cried.

I recalled Dennis saying, "What happened to that shy boy I knew in eighth *grade?*" and I wondered. My thoughts went back to Gifford's Park so long ago. That first kiss, summer school, Kathy, the boys bullying her. She even said I'd changed. *Change? Was it for the better? I learned to fly. I beat the McCaskey's. I got the girl of my dreams... and lost her.* I laughed cynically... *I'm going nuts...* I cried some more.

Mom used to pray for me all the time; and now she hates me. I've lost everything, even my mother. Maybe they are all right. I *am* a loser. Mom kept telling me to slow down, slow down, you have plenty of time. Dad was eager to think I was depraved; that I would attack Connie... and I almost killed her today; maybe he was right. "I am no better than Mac... a bully, arrogant and prideful." I sat against the tombstone and cried bitterly.

The sun was setting when I began to ride again. I went up Yokumtown Road to old York Road, still unclear where I was going. I heard loud music coming from the Farm, the notorious hangout off York Road, and turned in there. I recognized some cars... hot rods of a wide variety. Dennis's car was there, and I hesitated before entering.

The guys were in the game room, at a pool table. A low wall divided the game room from the dance floor and soda bar. There were a few teens dancing or gathered at tables near the front by the long bar and soda fountain. The game room was full. I did not see any of the guys looking my way and I slipped into the restroom at the back.

The Farm was a stable and barn. The bar, in the stable was called, logically, The Stable and served alcoholic beverages. The Stable was separated from the barn by a narrow gap with tables on an outside patio. The game room, soda bar and a large dance hall occupied the barn. The dance hall and soda bar were popular with teens. Local bands played there on weekends. It was quiet tonight, the juke box providing the music.

I washed my face and was drying it when Dennis came into the restroom. "Hey Michael. One of the guys thought he saw you. It's good to see you. How's it going?"

"I'm not doing too well at the moment."

"Yeah. I'm sorry we dragged you into our project. But I'm glad you were not hurt… in the crash I mean. Man, when we saw the plane falling like that, we thought you were dead, er… done."

"I didn't see you guys after the crash. I…"

"Yeah, those guys from the Army hustled us away and they wouldn't let us talk to anyone, not even to each other. It was a scary couple of days. We all wondered what happened to you. Nobody would tell us anything."

"They stuffed me in a room by myself and accused me of spying."

"Yeah." He laughed. "Go figure. I guess we were too close to the Aberdeen Proving Grounds. They test secret stuff there. Well, I'm glad you are ok. I would have called you, but my old man has kept me on a short leash. He wouldn't let me leave the house without him or Mom. This is the first night I've had to myself"

I grimaced, "How is your father taking your fall from grace?"

"He's blaming you, naturally. I tried to tell him *we* got *you* involved. But you know my old man… he never met a truth he couldn't ignore." Dennis shrugged. "He threatened to take my keys, but I need the car for work, so he backed off. I got my car back today. He would not be too happy that I'm here… if he knew. Hey the guys are in the pool room. Come on."

"You're eighteen. You are an adult now. You are supposed to be able to do your own thing. For better or worse."

"That may be so, but I still live in *his* house and eat *his* food, so I have to obey his rules."

"Uh-huh, well. I'm going to let you corrupt me." I greeted the boys at the pool table and looked around. "Someone buy me a bloody beer."

"Doesn't beer make you sick?" David asked.

"I could use a drink right now… it can't make me any sicker than I feel."

"You still getting grief from your parents?" Chuck said.

"It's a long story but Mom threw me out of the house tonight." I paused. "But enough about that. Things haven't been right between Dad and me since last fall. We don't talk much." I mumbled. "Buy me a beer and I promise I won't bring it up all evening."

"Done." Came a chorus of agreement, and David asked, "Why are you whispering? There are no cops here. You're old enough, aren't you?"

"Not until December. I'm seventeen... and a half." I laughed and looked around.

I joined them for a game of pool while Dennis went to get the beer. Dennis set the beer on a side table. I went to have a drink, but I found myself staring at the can and thinking about breaking rules. I decided to leave it... it did not go to waste.

The conversation wandered around touching on plans for the future... and girls. No one had seen Carol or Eleanor or Kathy or Pete since graduation.

"Did anyone see Connie before she left?" David said. "They left town in a hurry after graduation. I heard she was back in town."

Dennis said. "Her father was transferred. But I think she and her mother were in town this week."

I felt a moment of nausea thinking of earlier and I grumbled, "Who cares? She is a snitch, talking out of turn. She told the FAA about our test. Why worry about her?" I wondered what I was doing; why I was saying that. I knew my problems were not her fault. *Why am I still blaming her? Let it go Michael.*

"Whoa, Michael. That's not true." David said. "Woody called the cops. That was why he left early. He was mad because he was shut out of *his* project."

"Woody... called the cops?"

"Yeah. Connie didn't know where we were." Chuck said. "Unless you told her."

"No. No, I didn't tell her." I felt lightheaded and sick and abruptly headed for the bathroom.

I heard someone say. "Wow, that stuff *does* make him sick. He barely sniffed it."

I sat in a stall leaning on the wall sobbing. *Oh my God, what have I done? How could I be so stupid?* I thought about Connie, trying to remember what I said to her, but it made me vomit. I could not imagine how she must have felt. I wondered if she could ever forgive me.

I remembered her words, "I forgive you." And I wondered if she really could. I suddenly did not think I deserved to be forgiven. And Mom… how can I face *her?*

I was washing my face when David and Chuck found me.

"Hey what's up, Michael? You left in a hurry. We were worried about you." Chuck said. "Are you ok?"

"Yeah, what's up?" David said. "Does it have to do with Connie? I mean you looked like a ghost when I mentioned her."

I sat on the counter. "Yeah. I've made a real mess of things. Especially with Connie. It makes me sick thinking about it. I was blaming her and… and we had, uh words today. She came by the house. It went badly." *Badly hardly covers it* I thought.

"Well, you *have* been, uh… a bit… uh, insufferable…" Chuck winced as David poked him in the ribs.

But David added with a grimace and shrugged. "Arrogant might be a good word." He got a sharp look from Chuck.

I mumbled. "I guess I have been pretty much full of myself."

"Uh, yeah. Pretty much." David said. "I mean, you were doing great… with the flying, shooting, and fighting bullies like John and Mac…"

Someone yelled from the door. "There's a motorcycle gang outside. Looks like trouble. There is a big fight at the Stable. Everyone's leaving in a hurry."

As we came out of the restroom, Dennis rushed from the pool hall. "Hey, you guys better make yourselves scarce. Mac is here with a gang and he's yelling for Michael… and anyone who is his friend. I got out of there before he saw me."

"Oh crap, I'm riding my bike."

"Your bike? What happened to your truck?" Dennis said.

"I had to leave the house in a hurry… I didn't have my keys."

Dennis said. "Go out the back. I'll come around… if I can get to my car without being seen. We can go out the back road."

A parade of hot rods fled out the back road as the sound of chaos filled the night behind us. I saw flames coming from the Stable. "They are burning the place down. I hope there's nobody in there."

CHAPTER 28

"So, what are you going to do now?" Dennis said as we sped along the Valley Road. "You said your mom threw you out?"

"Yeah. I don't know. Maybe you can drop me off a little up the road. I'll see what happens."

"Is your little brother home?"

"No. He went up to Uncle Stephen's bible camp at the family lodge for the summer. He and my cousins, from Middletown, went up with Uncle Doug last Saturday. Maybe I should have gone with them."

"To bible camp?"

"Yeah. Maybe I could have used that, considering the mess I've made of everything. Mom wanted me to go, but, well..."

"I don't know. My mom and dad have never had much use for religion."

"Neither did I, at least for the last couple of years. It drove my mom nuts. And look at the mess I've made of everything. Maybe a dose of religion would have done me some good."

Dennis grunted and spoke. "What if they won't let you in the house?"

"I will have to figure out something. Maybe I'll go and camp on the river. My gear is all in the garage. I can start the truck without a key easily enough."

"What will you do for food?"

"Maybe I'll trust in God."

He laughed.

"I can trap rabbits and I have fishing gear with my stuff."

Dennis dropped me up the road from home. I spoke. "Maybe you should go home and lay low. Mac and his brother know we hung together. He may go looking for you. They know your car so maybe you should not be on the road."

"Yeah. I can't believe he brought that motorcycle gang just to look for you."

"He probably wants to remind the township of who he is and that he's still around. I did make him look foolish and ruined his reputation. I guess he figured it was *graduation* time for me." I grimaced and shrugged. "I'll see you, maybe in a week or so."

Dennis headed down the road to York Landing. I stood on the road looking at the darkened house. Nobody appeared to be home. I sneaked around to the back and found the emergency key by the basement door. I went to the garage and gathered my camping gear from the loft. I decided maybe I could use some stuff from the house, and I collected basic provisions from the kitchen pantry.

I decided to take some reading material and grabbed a novel about *Hornblower*, and my eye fell on that book, *Treasures*. Mom's bible was on the coffee table. I paused briefly and then stuffed both books in my haversack.

Having looted my parent's house, I prepared to head out of the garage when a group of motorcycles roared up to the driveway. "No-no. Why didn't I think that they would come here?"

The bikes pulled up at the foot of the driveway about forty yards from the house. A gang began to dismount.

I took my brother's 16-gauge shotgun and several boxes of ammunition from the cabinet… might as well be ready for anything. The darkened figures at the foot of the drive were backlit by the streetlight and I counted at least ten well-armed men.

I started the truck, being careful to engage the mufflers. I did not want any loud noise now. I left the lights off and threw the garage door open. I fired several shots in the general direction of the gang and watched them scatter.

I turned on the headlights, opened up the pipes and roared out of the garage. The motorcycles were blocking the driveway, so I crossed the lawn to our neighbor's driveway and out onto Valley Road.

A fusillade of gunfire struck the back of the truck and shattered the rear window next to my head. That was scary and I felt sick. I had not gone far down the road before I saw the lights of the motorcycles following. They were far behind as I topped the next rise and descended around a long curve toward York Landing. Just past the curve, I turned left onto an obscure side road that led down off the mountain to the river. I turned off my lights and descended to the road by the rail line.

John knew I worked at the boat shop, so I hid the truck among some pontoon boats and stacks of docks near Dietrich's. I hitched the trailer and the boat to the scooter, returned to the truck and loaded my gear into the boat. I found a tarp and covered the truck as best that I could. I was sure it would be enough so that no one would recognize the truck without looking closely. I was watching and listening for motorcycles, and I could hear them in York Landing in the Main Street Square a few blocks away.

I went up the river road to the York Landing Park and boat ramp and stashed the scooter and trailer in the brush next to the railroad after I launched the boat. I headed out onto the river as motorcycles approached the park on the river road. I saw their lights moving along the road and I turned downriver.

I mused, "The McCaskeys know I spend time on the river. I wonder if they will come after me. If they have gone to such an extreme to find me, they probably will not give up easily. They have access to boats, and they are not above stealing one. There were plenty of them at docks along the shore at this time of the year."

I went downriver past Shelley Island. There were people in their cabins on Shelley and some were still partying. I kept offshore, rounded the south end of Shelley, and landed on Beech Island, a small vacant island to the south. No one was on the islet, and it was quiet. I set up a rough camp in a secluded spot, intending to leave early in the morning.

All I could think about all night was Mom and Connie. I could not sleep thinking about them. The last time I had seen Mom she was sitting on the veranda looking dejected. I thought she must be so disappointed in me. I began to cry thinking about it.

In the morning before sunrise, I washed my face in the cold water of the river. I left the small island as the sun rose behind the trees on the east shore. I crossed to Tanner Island and hugged the shore hoping to hide in the deep morning shadows. I hoped that the dark green hull of my boat would blend in with the trees and brush on the shore. There were few boats on the river so early, just a few fishermen below Shelley Island, and upriver near Fall Island. I came even with the north end of

Tanner Island when a speedboat with four men sped up the east side of Shelley. I could see they were wielding long guns and I suspected it was Mac or his people. The boat disappeared behind Kohr Island.

As I came opposite Kohr Island the power boat came back. I was in the open and they apparently saw me. They turned toward me, and I turned into the narrow channel between Tanner and a small isle off the north end of the big island. My boat was not fast with the five hp motor and their boat had a large motor. They were closing rapidly, and I could not outrun them. I considered abandoning my boat and taking it to the shore.

But out of sight under the cover of Tanner, I pulled my boat up under overhanging trees and brush on the small isle. I removed the plug from the shotgun, loaded five rounds of birdshot, and waited.

The boat sped past, headed around the lower end of the isle. I waited, and shortly the boat came back, moving slowly as two men with rifles searched the shores on either side of the narrow channel.

I could hear them talking. "He has to be here, Dick. He was not on the other side."

"Maybe he took to the big Island."

There was more cover there and I hoped they would land and go searching. Then I could slip away. Maybe they would tangle with the guards on the island. After our project was exposed the company who now owned the island had posted guards. I listened.

"It will be hard to find him there and there are guards."

"Wait! I think I saw something… on that small island."

"You're crazy. Why would he go there?"

"Maybe because he thinks we would not look there. I saw a boat… I think."

Their voices echoed in the narrow corridor.

The boat turned back down the passage, moving slowly close to the shore. As close as they were they could not help but see my boat.

Someone yelled and they turned in toward my hiding place and the men began to shoot randomly into the bush apparently hoping to flush me out.

I crouched low as shots struck close, hitting trees and bushes near me. I was reluctant to shoot at them, but as they came closer, I decided I had no choice. I fired a couple of shots at the boat and watched them dive for cover. The boat turned away as I fired a few more shots close to them. Someone yelled, "We need to get Mac… and more guys."

"We don't need anyone else we have that punk trapped. He's not going anywhere." That sounded like Kane.

I crawled through the brush to near where the boat was idling in the channel. I stuffed three slugs into the magazine of the shotgun and aimed at the motor on the back of the boat. I fired three slugs into the motor and the transom. The motor blew the cover off and spurted flame as the boat went dead in the water, the transom tilted and threatened to fall off. The boat was taking on water, sinking as the crew frantically paddled for Tanner. I fired birdshot into the water behind them to encourage them. They crawled out onto the shore.

I launched my boat and went past the county marina on the east shore, threaded my way through the rocks and reefs and headed upriver. I did not see anybody following and no other boats on the river, so I slowed and caught some fish north of Hill Island before heading to Sassafras Island. There were still no other boats on the river, and I was certain I was safe for now. I concealed the boat and made camp in the trees away from the shore, opposite Little Stoney Island.

I sat back and relaxed in my hammock, shielded from prying eyes on the river and thought about everything that happened that day, and in the past month. In the quiet solitude of the river, I sat back and thought about Mom again. The image of her sitting on the porch stuck with me and I fought back the tears as they welled up inside me. When I tried to think of something else the image of me choking Connie came to me and I could not hold the tears back.

It was *my* fault. Everything that happened, the whole year came to a ruined heap, and it was all my doing. I felt guilty for not going back. I suddenly felt the need to pray but I did not know how to pray. I had forgotten; if I ever really knew how.

And anyway, why would God listen to me… why should he? I had ignored him for so long and had vowed I didn't need him. *Why would he listen to me now?*

I tried to read Mom's bible, but after flipping through the pages I didn't know where to start. There were notes all over, in the margins and inside the front and back covers with diagrams that I could not make head nor tail of. I turned to *Treasures* and re-read some of the verses that I had seen before. I decided to look up the bible references in Mom's bible and found my mother's notes in the margins. She mentioned the Roman Road and a bridge. I had no idea what she was talking about. She had written verses on the inside cover of the bible;

John 3:16 stood out. I heard that one mentioned a lot during our trip to Cape May. I tried to remember some of the stuff the reverend had said. *Repent* stood out.

However, the day passed quickly, and I went fishing for dinner. I had plenty of time to ponder what I had heard and read. I tried praying again but it was more in the way of a conversation with God. Person to person the same way I would talk to a person. I am sure I was irreverent.

"God, I know Mom trusted you, a lot. I don't know if you even want to hear from me. But Mom, well Mom is a good person. Don't punish her because of me, my foolishness, and my stupidity." I chuckled ironically, "Connie was right about that apparently. I think my mom is really disappointed in me. And Connie too. I was really terrible to her. She did not deserve that. I–I hope she will find it in her heart to forgive, *really* forgive me. I don't know what to do now."

I rambled on like that all afternoon, mumbling as I cooked dinner and cleaned up, saying whatever came to my mind.

"What is this 'Roman Road' that Mom mentions in her bible? Does it have anything to do with the Book of Romans?" I searched for mention of a Roman Road to no avail.

My search was interrupted by the sound of boats on the river late in the afternoon, but none came near my camp. However, being wary, the next morning, early, before daylight, I broke camp and moved upriver to an overgrown island above the turnpike bridge. After making camp I continued my search in the bible.

Mom had written references to verses under 'The Roman Road'. "Sure, Michael why don't you look up those verses, dummy." I muttered to myself.

I looked up the verses… they were all in Romans of course. I began to read through them in the order she had them written.

All have sinned… the wages of sin is death, but the gift of God is eternal life… God demonstrates his love… Christ died for us…whoever calls… shall be saved… if you confess… Jesus and believe… you will be saved… there is no condemnation for those who are in Christ Jesus.

I don't know why this did not sink in at first. Maybe I was just too dense. Or I thought it was all too easy.

There had to be something more. Some way for me to make up for the terrible things I had done.

I moved camp again, upriver to an island closer to Harrisburg just below the dam. I found another note in the back of the bible referring to 'The Bridge'. There was a diagram. Somehow that was easier to understand though now that I think about it there is nothing confusing about the Romans verses.

"We are separated from God by our sin. Because of sin God cannot… will not hear our prayers." That seemed contradictory to me. If he would not hear our prayers, how can we confess? The diagram showed Christ's cross bridging the gap between man and God. Something about that clicked in my mind and I thought I saw a glimmer of hope.

I was distracted preparing dinner, but I kept thinking about both the bridge and the Romans scriptures. I still could not put my finger on the idea that God will not hear me if I have sin in my heart. I was stumped but I continued to think about all of that. Another verse struck me; "Being justified by faith we have peace with God through our Lord Jesus."

My heart was troubled and frustrated as I sat in the hammock staring at the stars in the night. I knew I needed help to understand it all. I was not going to figure it out myself. That has been my problem; trying to figure things out by myself.

Frustrated and feeling lost I leaned my head against a tree. "God, I don't know what I am doing. I want to believe but I don't know what to do or what is going to happen to me. Please help me. Come and take control of my life and show me what you want me to do. I'm sorry for all the trouble I've caused. Please, help me to understand all of this."

I don't know how to describe what happened then. I had this feeling of well-being start in my breast and sweep over me; I smiled... I could not help smiling. And I knew... I knew I was going to be alright. Everything was going to be alright. I had a long way to go. I could not understand it all, but I just knew I was Ok. I could not stop smiling, I was filled with happiness... joy. I thought I understood what I had read; at least some of it. I was hungry to know more and to understand it all.

I was eager to get home and talk to Mom as I broke camp early in the morning. Maybe Mom could explain what it all means and help me understand. I cleaned up the camp and paused to read the book of Romans again. I began to read, and I read right through, going back to read some parts over. I was surprised that some of what baffled me before now made sense. I thought now I had a clearer sense of what

Jesus had done for me. A lot of it was strange and I had a lot to learn. I was eager to get started. I quickly packed the boat, shoved off, and headed down the river hoping to be home before nightfall.

CHAPTER 29

As I passed Spades Wharf Island I was thinking about the bible and the passages in Romans, and I was barely conscious of the boat approaching past Sassafras Island. I unconsciously steered right to give the other boat room.

I was startled out of my reverie when my boat shook from something slamming into it. I heard a bang, but it did not register. The boat shook and I turned my head to search the water alongside, looking for a rock or a piece of floating debris. Something struck my hat, the water erupted, and the crack of gunfire struck my ears. Bullets struck the boat showering me with water and splinters, whining by my ears and sending my heart into overdrive. I frantically looked around for the source and another bullet struck my hat. I was in a panic when I finally saw that the gunfire was coming from that boat I had ignored.

A familiar figure stood in the bow brandishing a rifle. I turned hard right toward the west shore and shelter as another bullet struck my hat. I got as low as possible in the boat and still see. Bullets continued to whizz by and strike the boat. I had no shelter; I had to get off the river.

I could not understand why Mac and his gang were still after me let alone how they knew where I was. I could not understand why they were so determined to get me. It had been nearly a week since the riot at the Farm and they were still coming after me.

The gunman's boat turned on a parallel path toward the west shore. I could hear Mac shouting and the burst from a machine gun shocked me as bullets tore at my wooden boat. They were going to blow my boat to pieces before I could get to shore.

They were going to cut off my escape and their boat was faster. Bullets rained all around me. I was not going to make the shore, so I turned back upriver. It made me feel sick to think about shooting someone but bullets tearing at the boat and my life jacket changed my mind. I fumbled with the shotgun, trying to load on the run and watch where I was going; I kept dropping shells.

Oh God why now? What have I done? You said to trust in you.

It did not occur to me that God was not punishing me. I still had a lot to learn. Nevertheless, I prayed, *God help me now, like you did with David with Goliath.* Yes, I do remember some stories from Sunday school. There was one where someone named Jonathan trusted you to help him and you did. Help me now, please.

I felt strangely calm, and I finally got five rounds into the shotgun. I tried to stop crying; I do not know when that started. *That would not be manly after all, would it? Men don't cry... do they? Was that a sin?*

I tried to zig-zag to throw off their aim. When the other boat drew alongside about twenty yards away, I turned sharply towards Spades Wharf Island. The other boat leaned sharply into a turn, exposing the men in the boat. I had a clear shot, and I sprayed the boat and its occupants with birdshot. John fell down in the boat and the others took cover, the boat swayed as the helmsman wavered.

Mac pointed a Tommy gun at me, and John stood up to shoot and then the boat hit an underwater obstruction. John flew off over the bow. Mac fell down and almost lost the Tommy gun over the side.

I headed across the river toward the air base at Olmstead. I looked for a place to land. The engineers had filled the river with rocks and gravel to build the new runway and the shore rose steeply from the water; there was no cover. I turned away from the base and tried to flee down river. The water erupted around me again and I was showered with splinters. The shooting was sporadic and not as intense. I looked back to see them pulling John out of the water while Mac continued to shoot.

A searing pain went through my side, and I dropped into the bottom of the boat. My terrors climbed with the pain and the blood spreading on my shirt. The sharp pain shot through me. I had never felt anything like it. Bullets hitting the boat disrupted my thinking. I lay in the bottom of the boat, hopefully out of sight but bullets passed right through the wood sides of the boat like through cloth. I could not see where I was going, and I poked my head up in spite of the bullets and looked over the side of the boat. I was headed for Little Stoney Island a hundred yards away. It seemed like a hundred miles with death stalking me. I had to do something about the pain and the bleeding.

The other boat had gotten free of the obstacle, and they were coming on after me. I headed for the channel between Little Stoney Island and Sassafras. There were trees and bushes down to the water on both islands. I had to do something about the bleeding. I darted behind Little Stoney and pulled my boat behind a pile of driftwood to escape another barrage of gunfire.

I took my pack and the gun and abandoned the boat, taking cover in the bush on shore. I tore frantically at my shirt, opened a dressing pack and pressed the dressing over the wound. I wrapped the Carlisle bandage around my waist. That did not lessen the pain. The pain made me cry. I was more scared than I ever had been. I thought that I was going to die, and I thought of Mom and the last time I saw her. It frightened me that the last thing I would remember would be choking Connie, and Mom chasing me from the house, and her sitting on the veranda as I pedaled away. I wanted desperately to see her again, to tell her how sorry I was.

I heard the other boat in the channel as it slowed; I stopped feeling sorry for myself. Men were getting off the boat on the upper end of the island and moving through the bush... they would find me soon. I went back to my boat. The pain in my side slowed me and I felt exhausted. I arrived at the dead fall as a thug came out of the brush in front of me.

"Ah, ha! I've got you! *He's here!*" He was as surprised as I was.

I swung the butt of my shotgun hastily and sent his rifle flying into the river among the driftwood. I tried to drive the butt of my shotgun into his face, but it glanced off his shoulder.

He stumbled backward yelling, "I found him. He's here, and he's wounded. He got my gun. Help!"

John appeared at the edge of the woods with a pistol. He fired and missed as I fell. I fired wildly and hit a dead tree near him. Wood splinters exploded around him and in his face. He screamed and ran back into the bush screaming that he was blind. I felt some satisfaction that I scared him, but hoped he was not seriously hurt.

I fell against the boat, exhausted. The wound was taking its toll. I pushed the boat away from the debris as Mac appeared in the channel.

I reloaded and pumped off several shots at the approaching boat. They turned and retreated back up the channel as Mac sprayed the shore and the deadfall with bullets. John, in the woods, screamed at his brother to stop shooting at *him*.

I got the motor started and headed for the intake channel at the power plant south of the air base.

Mac's boat shortly appeared from behind the island and took up the chase. He was alone with just his helmsman; he apparently abandoned his brother in his fixation on me. I was frustrated. I hoped that if I wounded some of them, they would give up.

I reached the shore near the power plant as his boat was nearly on top of me. I drove hard onto the shore and dove out as Mac came near and opened fire. I crawled up behind the boat and sheltered under the bow among some rocks as his barrage of bullets ripped at my boat. I could not go any farther... I was too weak. There was little cover, and I was shaking as I reloaded the shotgun with my last shells.

The gunfire stopped and I poked my head up. Mac was reloading machine gun, and I shoved the muzzle of the shotgun over the shattered gunwale and fired several shots, not aiming. He fell out of sight in the boat and the machine gun fell over the side. The helmsman powered the boat away from shore as I emptied my gun and collapsed in the brush by the bow of my ruined boat. I did not have the energy to reload, and I could still hear gunfire though it was not near me. I thought of lifting up to see, but just the thought seemed to sap my strength. Everything was hazy and I felt so tired. I wanted to sleep.

I heard shouting and I was dimly aware of being grabbed, jostled and moved. It was all a blur; I had no sense of time. Then I was in a vehicle, I was aware of bright lights and moving, and people yelling. Everything went blank.

CHAPTER 30

Mom was sitting by the bed with her head on my arm. Dad was napping in a chair across the room. "Mom." I put my hand on hers.

She looked up. "Michael."

"I messed up bad."

"You messed up badly." She corrected with a smile.

"Yeah, that too." I smiled. "Treasures."

"Treasures?"

"Yeah, Treasures. I finally figured out what you meant about laying up treasures on earth where they can be lost. Lay up treasures in heaven where no one can mess with them."

"Close enough, I guess. What have you figured out?"

"I tried to read your bible… oh I'm sorry… the boat was ruined. The bible was in the boat… and that book, *Treasures*… I took that too."

"We found them. They survived… and yes, the boat is ruined."

"I did a lot of praying this week. I think… and God answered. He said everything is going to be all right." I closed my eyes. "But he showed me that even though I'm ok with him he wants me to deal with the problems of life, with his help. I believe, now, that I can do that with him."

She brushed a teardrop from the corner of her eye, and she hugged me. Dad came and sat beside us. He had not been asleep but had been listening. "I have learned something too. I have not been a very good father… or a husband. I should not have been standing in the way when your mother tried to show you… us the way. I should have supported her… and you." He spoke sadly. "I wonder if you can forgive me."

I touched his hand. "Yeah. I can. I'm the one who needs to be forgiven. I'm sorry for all the trouble I caused. Is–is Connie still here?"

"No Dear, she left for the west coast with her mother last week."

"Oh. I really need to tell her how ashamed I am… of the way I treated her. She was right it was stupid… I was stupid and arrogant to think I could fly that plane. Everything I worked for… all my dreams… my treasures… I blew them all away because of my pride."

Dad said. "I've been doing a lot of thinking… without the help of the booze… about these past months and the way things got out of hand. I prayed and asked Jesus to be my savior years ago. But after the big war… then another war and more dead friends and Christians acting foolish… I let the things I saw turn me away from him and his church. I needed to be looking at the Lord, not people.

"I have been talking to some people and I realize now that we are all in the same boat, trusting our own feelings and not trusting in him."

"What happened… after I left the house? That motorcycle gang came to the house… when I left…"

Dad said. "I found your mother on the veranda, crying and praying. She told me about your fight with Connie."

"We prayed together." Mom said as she looked at Dad affectionately and touched his face.

"Then we went to look for you in York Landing." Dad said. "We went to see Dennis's father and he was not very friendly."

Mom said. "We talked to Elizabeth and Connie. They were just ready to leave. Connie did not tell her mother about the fight. I only told them we were looking for you.

"Connie said that she forgave you… she said that she saw something in your eyes… at the last second… before you left. She said she still felt some love for you, but she didn't think you would ever see each other again but she would always remember you fondly." Mom smiled and shrugged. "Forgive me if I entertained a mother's fantasy and hoped things would have worked out with you two. I would have been proud to have her for a daughter."

Dad said. "We went to York Landing and saw the boat at Dietrich's. Then we went to Valley view."

"We saw police cars heading up to old York Road," Mom said, "and we followed."

"There was a riot and a fire at the Farm." Dad said. "I don't think the council will have to worry about the Farm anymore."

"I saw your bike and after a discussion with the police we…" Mom said.

"Your mother used a ball bat to chase some thugs away from a girl and almost got us arrested. She demanded to talk to the kids they had rounded up."

Mom shrugged and rolled her eyes. "A couple of the local kids saw you there but said that you and some boys got out before the riot. One of them saw you in a Chevy hot rod.

"We thought that would be Dennis's car. We saw fire trucks on Valley Rd. They were headed for our house.

"Mr. Cramer heard the shooting and he saw one of them toss a fire bomb in the garage. He and Tom Mercer put the fire out before it spread. Tom's wife called the fire department and Tom is a volunteer firefighter. The garage was only slightly damaged." Dad said, "They caused some damage to the garage and broke some windows, but nothing that can't be fixed.

"Your truck and camping gear were gone, and we found your scooter at the launch ramp. It has been trashed."

Some of us went out to look around the islands. The guards had arrested Kane and some other thugs on Tanner Island." Dad said. "The police are still rounding up that gang."

A State Police detective came in to the room. "I am Captain Hadley. How are you young man?"

"I'm ok, now, I guess. Am I in trouble again?" I looked at Mom, worried. "I think I shot some people"

"With me? No." He chuckled looking at my mother.

"Did you catch Mac? Why was he so intent on getting me? How did they know where to find me?"

"The McCaskeys were associated with a Philly gang who were not happy that they were losing money in the central state area because Mac and Terry messed up, thanks to their vendetta against you. The Philly bunch wanted Mac to deal with the problem and they thought you were the problem. This debacle will put them out of favor with Philly.

"Officer Kane gave Mac a police walkie-talkie and they could listen to our broadcasts. They hid in a garage in York Landing. There was speculation that you had gone up river, and a boat was stolen last night. I'm sorry but we were slow to pick up on the connection between Kane, the thugs caught on Tanner's Island and you."

"You got Mac?"

"Yes. He and his driver were wounded. We found John and the other fellow on Little Stoney. He had a lot of splinters in his face and eyes. The other fellow had a broken hand and collar bone."

"You mentioned Terry."

"He was part of the gang, but he was still in jail in York because of the Valentine incident at McCormick's."

I laughed. "So, the Philly mob lost out because Mac and Terry could not forget a minor offence from grade school. Neat."

"It's always the small things that trip these fellas up."

"So, I guess that is the last I will see of the McCaskeys."

"What are your plans?"

"Join the navy, if they will let me."

"They should be glad to have you." He chuckled. "You are a fighter. Maybe you should join the Marines. They can always use a few good men."

I laughed, "Me? A marine? I'll pass. I've been shot at enough. I think I will join the navy and see the world."

The end… of the beginning.

www.ingramcontent.com/pod-product-compliance
Lightning Source LLC
LaVergne TN
LVHW021803060526
838201LV00058B/3225